The Making of Campaign
Strategy

The Making of Campaign Strategy

Marjorie Randon Hershey
Florida State University

Lexington Books
D.C. Heath and Company
Lexington, Massachusetts
Toronto   London

Library of Congress Cataloging in Publication Data

Hershey, Marjorie Randon.
  The making of campaign strategy.

  1. Campaign management. 2. Electioneering. I. Title.
JF2112.C3H47   329'.01   73-21757
ISBN 0-669-91330-8

Published simultaneously in Canada.

Printed in the United States of America.

International Standard Book Number: 0-669-91330-8

Library of Congress Catalog Card Number: 73-21757

To Howard

Contents

List of Figures

List of Tables

Preface

This study began in 1968. While working in a congressional campaign I found that much of what I had read about campaigning did not match my own campaign experiences. Journalists and scholars describe highly organized groups of people single-mindedly working to win. Campaigns that I was able to observe were quite different. They did not break any records for organization and unity. Rather, campaigns were fluid, changeable structures that were difficult to coordinate. Master plans would have seemed as out of place as an efficiency expert on the floor of Congress. Plans could be made to get out a mailing on a certain day, but there was no way to plan the accusations the opponent might make, which might be serious enough to require a new mailing. Perhaps there *are* campaigns that resemble computers, taking in information and putting out decisions and plans without so much as a folded or spindled IBM card. I have not seen one.

Another observation did not square with common knowledge about campaigns: writers tend to talk about the efforts campaigners make to persuade the voters; in reality a great deal of campaigning is directed toward satisfying internal needs, rather than checking on voter responses or seeking voter support. In fact, campaigns often operate without much input from the voters. I observed that canvassers and friends reported scattered bits of public opinion, but usually it was not organized and interpreted enough to be useful. Campaigners also heard about public opinion from party activists and people involved in other campaigns, but this information was not always reliable. However, the regular members of the campaign staff were in constant communication with one another, and it was they who provided the "public" reaction to a new leaflet or press release. It was often the expressed concerns of staff members, not the views of voters, that prompted other members of the staff to make changes in the campaign. Some activities were undertaken simply to impress the candidate or to perk up other staff members. Since people often act in response to cues from other people, and since campaigners did not receive many cues from voters, most of the cues that affected their activities came from within the campaign.

These observations provided a new perspective for looking at campaigns. Standing on the outside, it is easy to develop the image of a unified and coordinated campaign working at influencing voters. From the inside it becomes clear that campaigns, like other groups of people working toward a common goal, are small social and political systems with a diversity of beliefs, attitudes, and activities. Before asking how the campaign affects the voters, it is useful to ask what is affecting the campaign. To do so, we must look at the personalities, attitudes, skills and interactions of the people in charge. That is the aim of this book: to measure the impact of the perceptions and responses of the campaign's leaders on the campaign's external activities—activities designed to influence voters.

Many other aspects of campaigning deserve study as well. How, for example, do candidates and managers view their opponents? How realistic are their expectations about what an opponent will do, and about what the voters will do? What are the patterns of interaction and communication when a crisis occurs during a campaign? How much similarity is there between a candidate's contact with voters during a campaign and his representation of those voters during his term of office? Increased understanding of questions such as these would aid political scientists. And this information might also alert politically interested people to the potential uses and excesses of campaign organizations. Rather than having to depend on the courage of investigative reporters and judges, informed citizens might then become wiser and more cautious consumers of political campaigns.

I am grateful to many people at the University of Wisconsin and Florida State University for their help and advice. I have benefitted especially from the guidance of Austin Ranney. His adviserly talents were immensely helpful. Murray Edelman, Jack Dennis and Brian Silver all contributed insights to the development of the manuscript. Much-needed advice on data analysis was provided by Aage Clausen, Charles Cnudde and James Olson. Fellow graduate students at the University of Wisconsin also added to my understanding of politics. Although so many more deserve mention, my thanks go to Tony Broh, Marvin Druker, Barry Gaberman, Michael Kirn, Tony Mason, Bruce Oppenheimer, Robert Stover, and Richard Trilling. Charles M. Grigg, director of the Institute for Social Research, and Gilbert Abcarian, chairman of the Department of Government, both at Florida State University, graciously provided facilities and free time to enable me to complete the book. Barbara Rousseau and Deane Kessler deserve credit for helping with the typing.

Special thanks go to Congressman Robert W. Kastenmeier and his administrative assistant, Kaz Oshiki. Thanks are also due to the men and women who took time from their 1970 campaigns to help yet another political scientist understand what happens in the real world, out there beyond the university campus. Their patience and generosity was often remarkable. Reading the interview transcripts, one cannot help but appreciate the qualities of these campaigners—their dedication to principled politics, their enthusiasm, and the depth of their concern about the direction of American life. The interviews provided a fascinating array of settings, personalities, viewpoints and expectations. I wish that people who believe espionage and sabotage are "just politics" would have had the opportunity to observe this set of campaigns.

I am grateful to my parents, Lee and Helen Randon. Most of all, thanks are due to Howard V. Hershey. The marriage vows ask many things, but they do not even mention the requirement of spending long hours in the presence of tape-recorded politicians, even after the election is over, nor do they hint that a self-respecting biochemist might be so surrounded by legions of social scientists that even he begins to discuss the evening news in political science jargon. His ideas and suggestions are very much a part of this book, and his encouragement made it possible.

"It's hard being a campaign worker. We're completely at the mercy of our candidate. We do all the work and the candidate gets all the credit. We ring doorbells and make the posters and build up the candidate's image and then he says something stupid and ruins everything we've done! The next time I do any campaigning, it's going to be for myself."

—Lucy Van Pelt, campaign manager
for Linus Van Pelt
("Peanuts")

1 Introduction

It is mid-October in the election year 1970. The managers of two candidates for Congress, uncharacteristically, have put their activities on hold to reflect on the voters and the campaigns they are waging. They are located on opposite sides of the city, appropriately, for they represent opposing candidates and opposing philosophies of government. One sits in a congressional district office bedecked with the regalia of many years in Congress. The other struggles to find room for campaign materials on a desk, cluttered with the tools of his livelihood, that is resisting the intrusion.

The two men are radically different in their approach to politics. The race is locked up for the incumbent; both are aware of that. But the challenger's manager is fighting bitterly for a small share of the vote. With spurts of nervous energy and easy irritation, he speaks intensely about the voters in his district. He complains that the "noble" goal of educating the public during the campaign is a foolish idea. He states: "I don't have any question but that the time to get noble is *after* you're elected. If you get too noble *before* you're elected, you can be the most noble, continuously defeated person in the world." Standing outside the center of power, he comes directly to the point: "I'll be very honest. I think I'm a bit calloused and jaded in that I'm terribly disappointed with the level of sophistication of the electorate on a general basis."

The incumbent's manager, in contrast, relates his plans slowly and confidently, referring to the constituents with a parental concern. Yet he too agrees that voters are often apathetic and uninformed:

I can conceive of situations, perhaps remote but still possible, where efforts to educate the public in a really meaningful way can have negative repercussions that might cut into a candidate's vote, because to do that, you frequently have to delve into issues at some length and with some depth. The tragedy of course is that too few people are either willing or able to go into the issues that deeply, unfortunately.

These are disillusioned words for men whose jobs involve the promoting of political leaders to the public. They indicate that the campaign is not just a time when voters pass judgment on potential officeholders. It is also a period in which candidates, managers, and staff are learning about the interests, information, and responses of the constituents they hope to serve. The information that campaigners gain can be important. The assessments they make can affect their approach to politics and their performance in office.

1

As these two managers point out, at times the campaigner runs headlong into voter disinterest. He learns, as many political scientists have learned, that most voters tend to respond more to their party identification and to the familiar names of incumbents than to either candidate's qualifications for holding office.[1] What results from this learning? Or, put more broadly, what is the role of the campaigner and the campaign in the democratic process?

Campaigning is important in the life of a country. During campaigns, potential leaders must face their districts as a whole, rather than just those segments that take an active part in politics the year around. It is a time when enormous sums of money are spent, since most political money changes hands during the campaign period. It can also be a time of reassurance, allowing voters to feel that the system is functioning properly and victorious candidates to feel that their actions and policies have been right all along.

Most of all, campaigns are important because they are the ritual by which people in democratic societies choose their leaders. Studying campaigns provides information about the ways people achieve positions of power; it helps reveal the attitudes and behavior of these achievers; and it tells us how campaigners react to the views and demands of the voters.

Campaigning and the Importance of Leaders in Politics

A major reason for studying campaigns, then, is that campaigns are the road to political leadership, and political leaders in the United States exercise a dominating influence on political behavior. Agreement on this vital role of political leaders is widely shared among observers of American politics. In fact, one school of political thought, dubbed "elite theorists of democracy" by its critics, proposes that political leaders are the primary means by which democracy is maintained. These writers feel that popular rule is impractical in a large and complex industrial society. Therefore, since citizens cannot really govern themselves, they must instead be able to choose who will rule them. If citizens are allowed to choose among would-be leaders, and if those leaders are free to compete for popular support, this theory contends, the sufficient conditions for a democracy will be met.[2] One of the major spokesmen for this point of view, Joseph Schumpeter, points out that just as in economic activity, where producing a product is secondary to making a profit, the production of issues in democratic politics (and public involvement in producing issues) is secondary to the election of leaders.[3]

But the people still do rule in an indirect way, according to the elite theorists. When leaders must compete for public support, they know that if they do not represent public opinion they will probably be voted out of office. Competition has two benefits: it enforces democratic leadership and it brings out alternative positions on issues. As Frank Sorauf points out:

It is two *competitive* parties that provide the alternatives in candidates and issues on which a meaningful democratic choice depends. . . . The presence of the real alternative is as sharp a limitation, as sure a guarantor of responsibility in the political system, as it is in the economic marketplace.[4]

The vital role of elected leaders and candidates for leadership positions is underlined in this approach to democracy.

Other political theorists have criticized the view that the free choice of leaders is a sufficient definition of democracy. In the words of one major critic, the elite theories are a "revolt from the masses." This "revolt" represents disillusionment with the common man and the fear that many citizens are not fully in favor of minority rights, free speech, and other democratic principles. The result, Peter Bachrach writes, is a set of beliefs that turn traditional democracy inside out, finding benefits in an apathetic public and relying on a set of talented leaders to keep the polity on an even keel.[5]

In contrast, Bachrach believes that public apathy is *not* useful. Rather it is a danger signal, a sign that the political system is not doing its job. Democracy, he states, is not just a set of principles and outcomes favored by a majority of citizens. It is also a system of participation that, at its best, stimulates the human development of its members. It encourages the citizen to develop his capacity to "engage cooperatively in the solution of concrete problems affecting himself and his immediate community."[6]

The two groups of theorists evaluate modern politics differently. But they agree that political leaders rather than voters dominate American political life. As Bachrach puts it: "The exigencies of life in the industrial and nuclear age necessitate that key and crucial political decisions in a democracy, as in totalitarian societies, be made by a handful of men."[7]

A great deal of evidence suggests that leaders do control the defining of issues and the directing of government. One reason why political leaders and candidates are very important is that public interest in politics and government is relatively low, and there are not many other restraints on political leaders' ability to shape political life. Voters' interest in politics varies according to the issue involved and the nearness of an election, but even at the height of a presidential campaign the political concern of many citizens remains subdued. Information about the programs (and even the names) of many candidates is not widely distributed. One result is that incumbents have the edge over challengers in name recognition and resources, and consequently incumbents are likely to be returned to office. In 1970, 87 percent of United States congressmen were re-elected, typical of the normal re-election rate for congressional incumbents.[8] With the knowledge that they are likely to be re-elected, incumbents can be less bound by the fear that ignoring the voters' preferences will result in election defeat.

Even two-party competition does not always ensure that the public can control its leaders. V.O. Key has proposed that the two parties do have different centers of gravity on issues, and when people switch their votes from one party to the other, they do so generally in order to move closer to the issue positions they believe in.[9] But many people are not concerned with switching their votes. They have identified with a party since early in life, well before they knew what their party stood for,[10] and their continued identification does not depend on their party's positions on issues.[11] So in many areas candidates are elected largely because they bear the majority party's stamp of approval, not because they have learned and espoused the wishes of the voters. One Wisconsin campaign manager described the party loyalists of his district in these terms:

About 25 percent of the people in this district would vote for Donald Duck on the Republican party [ticket] and against Jesus Christ on the Democratic party, and there are another 25 percent who would vote for Mickey Mouse on the Democratic party and against the Holy Ghost on the Republican party.

Political leaders are rarely held on a short leash by their constituents. Therefore, leaders have a lot of latitude in deciding how they will represent the public. Several researchers have reported that political leaders themselves believe that they are relatively free to define their roles and that voters can be persuaded to accept these definitions. Lewis Anthony Dexter has capably pointed out that elected officials even define their *constituencies* for themselves.[12] They hear the voices of some groups more clearly than the voices of others. In this way, some groups in the constituency gain greater influence because they have the ear of their representative while others do not.

Many representatives feel that their own judgment on issues is more reliable than the changing and semi-formed opinions of their constituents. A four-state study conducted in the late 1950s found that between 55 and 81 percent of those states' legislators chose the role of "trustee" (independent interpreter of the district's best interests) rather than that of "delegate" (representative instructed by the voters) or a combination of the two roles.[13] A study of a sample of U.S. congressmen in 1963-64 found a much smaller proportion of admitted trustees but still uncovered a deep streak of independence. Only 32 percent of the congressmen interviewed agreed with the view that "a Representative ought to work for what his constituents want even though this may not always agree with his personal views."[14] The observer can conclude that most of the people we elect to office do not believe their only purpose is to learn what the majority of their constituents are thinking and then carry out those ideas. Instead, most elected officials are responding to other conceptions of representation. One of these conceptions is that the political leader makes an effort to determine the nation's needs, and after consultation with interested parties (including voters) he tries to get his views adopted.

Of course there are many cases in which public outcry has forced an elected official, or even an official who does not depend on elections for his job, to back down. A case in point is the deluge of telegrams that flooded the White House after the "Saturday night massacre" of October, 1973, when President Nixon fired Watergate Special Prosecutor Archibald Cox, Deputy Attorney General William Ruckelshaus, and accepted the resignation of Attorney General Elliot Richardson who resigned in protest. The White House, startled by such strong public reaction, felt compelled to provide the courts with the presidential tapes that Cox had been seeking, and to name another special prosecutor. But these levels of public outcry are rare. And when public reaction to an official's decision falls short of massive proportions, it is often left up to the official to characterize the reaction. Accordingly, telegrams from his district may be reported as pressure-group mail, or simply a "temporary outcry" caused by the official's failure to explain fully why his decision was the only one possible.

Because political leaders are central to the quality of American politics, they are able to sway public opinion. Elected officials make news. They can call upon the symbols of political authority to command voters' loyalty. There are many notable examples of issues on which a political leader's action has caused public opinion to follow.[15] Therefore it is important to learn more about political leaders—how they go about making decisions, whom they listen to, what values they hold, what personality characteristics they have that might bear on their decision-making. The fewer controls we can find on the actions and attitudes of elected officials, the more vital it is to find out as much as possible about the officials themselves.

During the relatively brief life of a campaign, candidates—even those who are not elected—make their mark on public opinion. The activity of George Wallace in the 1968 presidential campaign sharpened the law-and-order issue as an important political question. The enthusiastic 1968 primary campaign of presidential contender Eugene McCarthy raised many people's consciousness with regard to the Viet Nam war. Because campaigns generate a certain increase in political interest through news coverage of political leaders, they can indeed make a difference in the way issues are defined.

But more than raising or clarifying issues, campaigns matter because they are the stage on which political leaders rise to power or fall into the shadows. In a hypothetical representative democracy where elected leaders function as cameras conveying the exact shape of district opinion into some decision-making machine, it would not matter whether candidate A won or candidate B lost. In the American political system, however, it is difficult for leaders to learn what district opinion is and even more difficult for the public to find leaders who are willing to convey that opinion without interpreting it. Therefore the kinds of leaders that are elected—their values, their personalities and their abilities— influence the direction of American politics. Campaigns provide and condition the leaders who will direct political life. But what actually happens in a campaign? What kinds of people run for public office? What influences affect the campaigners' decisions? What must a candidate do in order to win?

What Happens in Campaigns

Writers have assumed that there are many commonalities among campaigns. One assumption is that the goal of a campaign is to win the election. Campaigners whose positions seem hopeless may decide that they can only hope to educate the public on some important issues or dramatize certain ideas. But even many candidates who are serving as sacrificial lambs still aim for victory. The question is not whether victory is accompanied by sufficient voter education to be acceptable, but how victory is to be attained.

The would-be leader is faced with many major tasks, which can be performed in many different ways. The first—often the hardest—is to recruit a hard-working organization to support the candidacy. Generally this organization is led by a campaign manager, in theory the alter-ego of the candidate. The manager is usually expected to take care of the administrative, scheduling, and personnel matters so that the candidate's time can be spent meeting voters and gathering support. The manager, again in theory, has all the qualities of a good hunting dog. Above all, he is loyal. He knows his business, keeps his concentration, is always available, intelligent, and willing to follow through. Also like a hunting dog, he has the dubious distinction of winning a prize for someone else's enjoyment. An experienced campaign consultant describes his "inflexible rule for campaign managers" this way: "If the candidate wins, it is because of his charm, intelligence, and appeal to the voters; if he loses, it's your fault."[16] Beyond the manager, campaign organizations vary in the number of specialists they utilize and the numbers of volunteers they attract. The specialization of function and degree of organization also vary, but most campaigns are thought to require at least a minimal amount of organized manpower.

Second, campaigns are likely to need outside support. The most important kind of outside support is financial—contributions, loans, gifts in kind, and salaries. Since in most campaigns it is virtually impossible for the candidate to meet every constituent—or even a majority of constituents—to seek support, methods of mass communication are crucial for reaching voters who would not otherwise be contacted; and most media for mass communication, when used over a large area, wear price tags that can be dazzling. Outside support for the campaign is also needed in the form of endorsements, since endorsement by a respected group or person may sway some voters who value those opinions. In addition, endorsements often carry the promise of financial support, which is a welcome sound to the ears of any campaigner.

Third, campaigners face a choice of priorities. With a large district and a small amount of time, it soon becomes apparent that gaining the support of some groups or areas is of higher priority than others. What groups or areas will play this crucial role depends very much on the way a candidate estimates his likely support. If potential support in the district is high, then the campaigner can win by locating those supporters and getting them to the polls. If potential support is low, groups that ought to be susceptible to the candidate's charms must be identified and wooed. If the candidate is well-known in some areas and unknown in others, he must decide whether he can win by going with his strength, or whether he must risk ignoring his supporters in order to make an impression on those strangers.

Three additional campaign tasks can be grouped together because they form what could be called the substance of the campaign. These include making the candidate's name known to the voters, getting across a desired image of his character and ability, and publicizing his stands on certain issues. In the abstract these would seem to be quite different activities. Name-recognition might be achieved by billboards, bumperstickers, or buttons; an image campaign might be conducted by putting the candidate on television for short spot advertisements; and issues might be promoted through press releases to newspapers and supporters. But in practice these three types of campaign activities overlap. When a candidate pays for a billboard that proclaims "Vote for Safer Streets— Elect Snort," he has touched all three bases. A short message—six words—assures that his name will be perceived by passersby. The name, further, is associated with an issue. The issue of safer streets calls forth in the reader's mind several notions that the candidate hopes are stored there: notions about the rise in criminal activity, fears about personal weakness, a desire to protect possessions. This candidate, then, is following the advice of campaign consultant Joseph Napolitan and promoting an issue by triggering responses from the voter's memory, rather than giving the voter a lot of new material to learn (the latter being more difficult and more expensive).[17] And the linking of this issue with the candidate tells the voter some things about the candidate's character. He is probably dynamic (he keeps his messages to the point) and tough (concerned about crime).

Once all these decisions are made, a choice of weapons is necessary. Television, radio, newspapers, direct mail, bumperstickers, matchbooks, student canvassers, aerial balloons—all have had their proponents. Which of these methods are used probably depends upon many factors: the physical characteristics of the district, the types of appeals chosen, and the groups to which the appeals are directed. In a suburban area, for example, television and radio appeals are often inefficient. The stations are likely to reach an entire metropolitan area, and despite the satisfaction gained by informing millions of people about one's good points, few candidates see much benefit in paying for all of New York when all they really need is Brooklyn. And it is often assumed that a campaigner would be likely to choose different media for appealing to blue-collar workers than to professional people. While television advertising might best reach the former, advertisements in particular magazines might attract the latter's attention more efficiently.

Last, the campaign needs feedback. It is assumed that campaigners must have information on how particular appeals are working, how the trend of voter preference is going, and how well the campaign's targets are being reached. Information can be gathered through polls or canvassing, from trusted sources such as friends and party leaders, from supposedly impartial sources such as the press, or simply from their own "feel" of the situation.

These tasks are considered common to all campaigns. The way each task is done and the level of efficiency involved varies widely. Differences in the style of campaigning have been attributed to the resources available, the size of the constituency, the credits the candidate may already have with groups of voters, and the personal capacity of the candidate and his staff. For instance, some candidates tend to campaign more actively than others. In addition to their estimates of how much campaigning is needed, candidates' activities may depend on their personal ability to tolerate long hours of voter contact. The point is illustrated by the responses of four 1970 candidates to a question about the amount of active campaigning they do. First, compare two challengers, both very likely to lose. One says, "Planning strategy is a twenty-four-hour job. I spend most of my time here planning strategy. Going out is a sideline." Another describes his efforts in quite different terms. While the first candidate is quite reserved, this man is brimming with optimism.

The primary area will be myself. I will be doing a substantial amount of personal campaigning, which I feel is the greatest asset of a campaigner. Especially in an area like this where the chances are three to one against me, the only way I'm going to stand a chance is to actually get face-to-face with as many of the voting people in my area as possible.

Different approaches to active campaigning are also expressed by two incumbent congressmen, both assured of victory. One points out that his time for active campaign work is limited because Congress stays in session till October in an election year. But he adds:

Frankly, I don't object to it, because I think that a grueling three to four months on the campaign trail is enervating in a sense—intellectually enervating. You just get to the point where you can't think of anything new to say, and all you do is keep repeating old speeches to service clubs.

However, another congressman with similar resources and similar support states:

Oh, I suppose every person in public office dreads the prospect of another campaign. But once you get into it and the give and take starts, it's kind of like the old firehorse—it's not really unpleasant at all. I enjoy working the shopping centers and walking up and down the streets.

Thus, candidates in similar positions often run different kinds of campaigns. To find out why, it is necessary to examine several factors that influence the running of campaigns.

Many aspects of campaigns have been studied in the past. Authors have addressed themselves to questions such as these: How is political money sought and contributed during campaigns?[18] What strategies are available to contenders in presidential nominating conventions?[19] How has the advent of the New Politics affected campaigning in America?[20]

The question "What influences campaigners to approach the voters and make decisions the way they do?" has also concerned many students of politics, and has produced many answers. These answers fit into three broad categories. Some answers have to do with the conditions of the political system in which the campaign is conducted. Others involve "external" characteristics of the campaigners themselves, such as incumbency, party, and occupation, and still others have to do with "internal" characteristics—the attitudes, perceptions, and personality traits of the persons involved.

In the first category, many areas of campaign decision-making have been thought to respond to the political environment of the campaign. Traditional wisdom tells us that candidates run harder at general election time in two-party competitive areas than in one-party areas, and that in one-party systems where factionalism is dominant, candidates are likely to need their own organization rather than expecting to rely on the party's efforts.[21] The uncertainty of campaigning is also thought to affect campaigners in several ways, causing them to work harder,[22] to be more responsive to the opinions of the voters,[23] and to cling to traditional campaign methods.[24]

In the second category, incumbency is thought to be a powerful influence on campaign decisions. According to one study, incumbents tend to have more information available to them about issues and voters' views, more sources of funds and campaign volunteers, and a greater likelihood of support from other groups. than challengers do.[25] Party, other authors say, affects the kinds of decisions made in campaigns. Nelson Polsby and Aaron Wildavsky state that since Republicans are members of a minority party, they must gear their efforts to independent voters and wavering Democrats as well as to Republican faithful, or else they must blur party differences with some overriding attraction. In contrast, the majority Democrats must concentrate on turning out their own party identifiers.[26]

Finally, a few writers have suggested that the personality of a campaigner will lead him to choose certain approaches to organizing a campaign and influencing voters. Aggressive personalities would be likely to choose an aggressive approach to their constituents. Rigid personalities might lean toward a highly structured chain of command in their organization, rather than a more flexible, less organized staff.[27]

Campaign Organizations:
Disciplined or Diffused?

Many authors have devoted their attention to the campaign organization itself. Traditionally, commentators on American politics have discussed election campaigns as though they were military operations. We hear about campaigns as "fights," "guerrilla operations," "clashes," and about campaign preparations as "logistics" and "battle plans," carried out by "troops" of volunteers. It is not surprising that many people, including prominent writers, tend to think of a candidate's organization as a military unit, tightly organized, responding to authority, and highly unified.

This view is often seen in the writings of one seasoned observer of presidential campaigns, Theodore H. White. He describes campaign organizations as command structures, obeying orders from the top. In his account of the 1968 presidential race, for example, he writes:

About Nelson Rockefeller . . . All across the country, thousands of Rockefeller well-wishers, hundreds of politicians had been waiting to hear the trumpet call to battle.

About Gene McCarthy . . . New Hampshire is Republican. On the Democratic side of the political ridge, McCarthy's student commandos are preparing to groin the President of the United States.

About Lyndon B. Johnson . . . Lyndon Johnson, too, on this Tuesday, was on the telephone to his deputy, Marvin Watson, urging Watson to flog the Southern governors into line for Humphrey in order to stop Kennedy. By late afternoon the Southern breakaway from Humphrey had collapsed.[28]

Textbooks on American government and descriptions of the New Politics reinforce this concept of the unified campaign. They often refer to the election activities of the candidate or the party, when they are actually describing the work of the campaign staff as a whole. This assumes that research centers on the candidate because his staff is an outgrowth of his own mind and intentions. Yet others have pointed out that chaos, rather than military discipline, is characteristic of many campaigns. Comparing a campaign organization to a military unit is somewhat akin to comparing a football team with the football fans as they empty the stadium after the game. Describing a presidential campaign, V.O. Key explains:

In truth, the campaign organization is a jerry-built and makeshift structure manned largely by temporary and volunteer workers who labor long hours amidst confusion and uncertainty. Assignments of responsibility and lines of authority are likely to be hazy. The army of campaign workers is loosely articulated and some of its regiments may be sulky, if not actually insubordinate.[29]

In short, as one campaign adviser admonished a political scientist, "the trouble with most analyses of political behavior by political scientists is that they attribute a reasoned working out of things which are not worked out reasonably."[30]

Conflict can be found between the campaign staff and party regulars,[31] between volunteers and the people responsible for organizing them. But further, observers can find many differing viewpoints within the candidate's staff itself.[32] Many such conflicts were found in the 1970 Wisconsin campaigns. As an example, let us look at one of these campaign organizations, different from those discussed early in the chapter. First, this was an extremely close race. Up until election day, seasoned political hands in Wisconsin were not giving odds on who would win. And second, this was a high-budget, well-staffed campaign, in contrast to the more modest budgets of a shoe-in or a sure loser.

The candidate, feeling the pressure of a full schedule of speeches and meetings, speaks amiably, but the listener detects a note of discontent. When asked what he dislikes most about campaigning, the candidate answers quickly:

Hacks. People who think that the fact that you come to talk to them says you have to do what they want you to do. I really don't like that. What's the sense of getting to a place and then having so many obligations that you aren't free to do what you think you should?

His manager, on the other hand, is not worried about hacks. He is worried about candidates. The executive of a business firm, this manager has directed many campaigns in the state. He sees himself as a very practical man with an instinct for successful electioneering and a growing knowledge of the effectiveness of different campaign methods. But when mentioning exchanges of views with other experienced party workers whom he trusts, he does not mention the views of his candidate. Speaking generally, he describes what the role of a candidate should be:

The candidate should concentrate on the uncommitted—but it takes quite a bit of discipline and intelligence for a candidate to be able to identify an uncommitted voter. Too often, when he thinks he's talking to an uncommitted, he is really talking to someone who's committed the other way. . . . Usually the candidate doesn't have a very good grasp of what's going on otherwise [without the guidance of his staff]. He's too likely to be influenced by everyone he runs into.

Another campaign manager reported a comment that sums up this man's views even more concisely: "It was a Friday afternoon. We were all just dead, and we were having a few problems with some of the candidates already, when [the first manager] said, 'you know, campaigning would be a lot of fun if it weren't for those damn candidates.' "

The internal warfare (to borrow another military analogy) indicated by these remarks can be found in all types of campaign organizations. Differences between candidates and managers range from simple disputes over tactics to basic disagreements about the place of political issues in campaigning, and about the relative competence of one another's performance. Surprisingly clear differences exist between candidates and managers in their perceptions, goals, personalities, and decision-making. Often managers do not arrive at the same decisions as their candidates, nor in the same ways.

It is, therefore, a major finding of this book that campaign organizations are rarely similar to unified and highly controlled organizations. This interpretation of campaigns has several consequences in the understanding of political organizations:

1. Instead of viewing the campaign staff as an outgrowth of the candidate, it is better seen as a social system—a miniature political system in which power is diffused, coordination is difficult, and mass participation, as with the nation, is limited. Once inside this small system, much can be learned about the vectors of power and about the organizational influences on a campaigner's ideas and activities.

2. Perceptions and concerns of the candidates and the managers form two clear and different patterns.

3. So many candidate-manager differences will be demonstrated that the assumption that a candidate's views and behavior represent the campaign as a whole will be shown to be very hazardous.

In specific terms, many differences between candidates and managers are areas for investigation. Are managers, as well as candidates, concerned with hearing the views of the voters and other groups? Might the managers be even more responsive to public opinion than the candidates are? Or are the managers the crafty, shady political manipulators found in smoke-filled rooms?

Who runs the day-to-day operations of the campaign? Does the candidate spend time inspiring the volunteers to greater effort, or is it the manager who takes primary responsibility for internal activities? Which role is more flexible, more adaptable to changes in the campaign situation? Is the candidate able to change his approach as the circumstances of the campaign change, or does he rely on the manager to set his direction? What questions are candidates and managers most likely to disagree on: the target of their appeals? the kinds of campaign techniques that should be employed? Are there certain methods typically favored by candidates and typically opposed by managers? All these questions will be discussed, and reasons will be suggested for differing orientations. The result, it is hoped, will be a greater understanding of the political activity involved in the attempt to gain leadership positions in America.

In summary, this book will examine the influence of personality and perceptions on campaigners' activities and beliefs. The effects of several factors will be traced. First, the amount of uncertainty the campaigners see in the campaign environment will be investigated. Does uncertainty lead them to be more responsive to constituents, for example? Characteristics of the campaigners will be studied, such as their party identification, occupation, incumbency, and their position—candidate or manager—in the campaign. Three elements of the campaigners' personalities and attitudes will be measured. The first is a personality trait that seems a likely candidate for hampering responsiveness: intolerance of ambiguity. Perhaps campaigners who do not like ambiguous situations are less adaptable to campaigning and meeting voters because they must remain in the dark about the voters' ultimate judgment until election day. Second, the amount of stress the candidates and managers feel may enhance or reduce their capacity to respond to the public. And finally, their theories about the way a campaign should be run may affect their decisions.

A number of campaign decisions will be tested to see if they are affected by the above factors and in what ways. One group of decisions involves responsiveness to the views of voters, contributors, and other groups. Decisions in this category include the sources that are tapped to learn public opinion, where funds are raised, whether professionals in campaign management (such as advertising agencies) have a voice in campaign policy, and how flexible the campaigners are in adapting their tactics, issues and personnel to new information about the campaign situation. The second group of decisions is organizational: how the campaign staff is recruited, how formal or informal are the lines of communication within the staff, how morale is maintained, what media or other techniques are used in campaigning and to what extent.

The Setting for Research

To undertake such an analysis, this study focuses on campaigns in the state of Wisconsin during the 1970 election year. Because there was no presidential contest in 1970, the candidates and their organizations can be seen in clear relief, without the dominating impact of the presidential campaign. Persons running for Congress and for the five statewide offices in Wisconsin (governor, lieutenant governor, secretary of state, treasurer and attorney general) were interviewed during the election period—late August to that fateful first Tuesday of November. Offices below the level of Congress and statewide positions were not included because other surveys of political candidates, most notably John Kingdon's study of an earlier Wisconsin election, indicated that most candidates for state legislative and lower-level offices did relatively little campaigning, and did not spend much time working out a structure of perceptions about their campaigns.[33]

To examine the nature of politics in a given state is an interesting and useful task, but it gains added value if the conclusions reached can be placed in a more general context in order to suggest hypotheses about American politics in general. Comparing Wisconsin with other states allows an estimate of the generalizability of this study. Therefore, some essential features of Wisconsin politics will be identified to provide background on the conditions campaigners must respond to in that state, as a basis for comparison with other areas of the country.

Wisconsin, like most states, has many different political subcultures. For example, two congressmen represent the city of Milwaukee, a metropolitan area of 1.4 million persons (in 1970) that includes most of the black residents of the state. Other congressmen are elected from sprawling rural and small-town districts in which the primary issues are farm bills and flood control. But two general themes dominate the nature of Wisconsin politics. First, the state has had a long tradition of limited party politics, fueled by strong negative feelings toward powerful party organizations. And second, Wisconsin has moved from the Republican column into lively two-party competition at the state level. The party battle lines are drawn like those in other two-party states, with Democrats drawing their strength from metropolitan areas and large cities while Republicans dominate smaller cities.

Opposition to strong parties, however, is rampant. The Wisconsin parties closely resemble the amateur political organizations of California and New York. The amateur nature of Wisconsin politics does not imply that Wisconsin politicians do not make public office their professional career. On the contrary, seven of the state's ten congressmen in 1970 had been in Congress for at least ten years, and all but one of the candidates studied had extensive political experience prior to 1970.

But amateur politics *does* imply that instead of highly organized local political units concerned with patronage, these campaigners must face the conflicting demands of local leaders who are likely to be professional or business-managerial persons and housewives, who are oriented toward state and national rather than local issues.[34] These kinds of demands are probably harder to satisfy than the pragmatic requests for jobs and contracts that characterize machine politics. They help explain why Wisconsin politics is often considered more issue-oriented than politics in many other states.

Campaigners in Wisconsin also face a fluid competitive situation. They must run as individuals rather than rely on the efforts of a strong party organization. This lack of party strength is well described by a campaign manager recently transplanted from a strong party state:

When I first came up here and saw how they ran politics, campaigns, I told some people, "Some weekend a couple of Chicago politicians are going to come up here and see what's going on, and they'll come up the next weekend and take over the whole state. And you won't even know it's happening."

Wisconsin is one of the few states to have an open primary, resulting in the interesting (and highly unpredictable) phenomenon of party identifiers having an opportunity to choose the opposition party's candidates. This crossover voting often occurs when one party primary provides little or no competition while a hot fight is taking place in the other column. Consequently, Wisconsin candidates must be especially attuned to independent and opposition party voters, even in the primary election.

Over the last four decades a marked change has occurred in Wisconsin politics. Leon Epstein, chronicling state political patterns, notes that from 1900 to 1932, "Wisconsin politics were fought largely within the Republican party," with the conflict occurring between the Progressives—the spiritual heirs of Senator Robert La Follette—and the more conservative Republicans.[35] But between 1944 and 1957 Wisconsin Democrats made their move, organizing statewide, and finally reaping the fruits of their labor with the 1957 victory of William Proxmire, ironically, to fill the Senate seat of the late Joseph McCarthy. The 1964 state reapportionment of congressional districts further cemented two-party competition in Wisconsin.[36]

The Wisconsin campaigners now face a constituency that is generally typical of two-party states. Austin Ranney has suggested that such states tend to be more urbanized, and to have higher median incomes, a higher proportion of foreign stock, and a lower proportion of the labor force in agriculture than do one-party and modified one-party states.[37] Wisconsin is predominantly an urban state, although it lacks the sprinkling of large industrial cities that typify Northern competitive states. The state's median income is somewhat higher than the national median income, and Wisconsin, while its proportion of foreign stock does not exceed the national average, has been the site of migration of a large German population that has influenced the nature of state politics for many years.

There are some exceptions to this two-party pattern. Wisconsin's population is more weighted toward agriculture than most two-party states, and its black population is much smaller. Only 3 percent of Wisconsin's residents are black, compared with 11 percent nationally. However, Wisconsin's black population grew by 72 percent during the last decade—compared with a 20 percent increase nationwide—so that the issues of race can be expected to have a part in state politics. But in many ways Wisconsin's population resembles the socio-economic mix of most two-party Northern states. There is reason to believe, therefore, that the political environment of this group of campaigners is not unique to Wisconsin, and that the conclusions to be drawn here about Wisconsin politics apply more broadly, as hypotheses, to American two-party politics in general.

Coming into the 1970 election, the campaigners faced sets of issues that were found in most states. Looking at Wisconsin's seventh congressional district, for example, *Time* magazine found "a microcosm of American political concern and action in 1970."[38] The issues here revolved around the economic downturn, rising taxes, and the broadly-termed "social issue"—the constellation of racial unrest, violence, social change and personal insecurity so insightfully analyzed by Richard M. Scammon and Ben J. Wattenberg in *The Real Majority,*[39] a handbook for many of these candidates in 1970.

Republican campaigners in Wisconsin and elsewhere, spearheaded by the active campaigning of Vice-President Spiro Agnew, attempted to associate the Democrats with violence and radicalism—to put them on the wrong side of the law-and-order issue. This use of the social issue was especially relevant in Wisconsin where concern had long been generated by student protests at the large and distinguished state university in Madison. Concern reached a peak after a bombing that cost the life of a university researcher just prior to the beginning of the 1970 campaign.

On the Democratic side, the main theme was also national in origin. One reporter, describing the defeat of the Republican candidate for governor, wrote: "the vote against Olson was probably not directed against his candidacy for governor as much as it was directed against the economic policies of President Richard Nixon's administration."[40] Particularly disturbing to Wisconsin Democratic campaigners were the problems of high property taxes, high interest rates, high unemployment, and high prices.

When the campaign began, Democrats held four of the state's ten congressional seats but none of the five statewide posts. Tradition would lead campaigners to expect that the congressional incumbents would have the edge, and that the current balance would be maintained. In 1968 the average winning percentage for the Wisconsin congressional races, typical of the decade, had been 64 percent and all ten incumbents were returned to their seats. Thus in 1970, interest was concentrated on only two of the congressional contests: one had been a marginal seat throughout the 1960s, and the other involved a spirited Republican challenge to a first-term Democratic incumbent, who had narrowly won the seat after its former occupant, Congressman Melvin Laird, resigned to become Secretary of Defense. The national Republican party saw the 1970 race as their last chance to regain this seat, before the Democrat's growing congressional experience made him harder to beat.

In contrast, the statewide elections in Wisconsin have traditionally been cliff-hangers. As in most states, the statewide officers represent a larger and more heterogeneous area than do congressmen and therefore tend to be more vulnerable to currents of public dissatisfaction. For example, only one of the five offices had averaged more than 55 percent of the vote for the victor and only one office had been held by the same party throughout the decade beginning in 1960. Further, in 1970 a popular Republican governor was retiring, and Democrats felt that the Republican lieutenant governor, attempting to move up, was a weaker candidate. The state contests were thus expected to be closely fought.

Early indications that the economic issue would dominate, to the advantage of the Democrats, proved true. Democrats picked up the two spotlighted congressional seats, and pared the usually comfortable margins of two other Republican congressmen to 51 and 52 percent. Three of the statewide offices also fell into Democratic hands; the governor, lieutenant governor and treasurer each captured his position for the Democrats with less than 54 percent of the two-party vote.

This Democratic victory was national in scope. Democrats took a net gain of 11 governorships from Republicans in 1970, the largest gain in governorships by either party since 1938. Democratic gubernatorial candidates in 1970 garnered a million-vote plurality over Republicans, and the Democratic margin in the House of Representatives was fattened by nine. This change is characteristic of off-year elections. Every year since 1934 there has been a rebound from the presidential party, and in 1970 the rebound was substantial. However, the traditional safety of most congressional seats was maintained in Wisconsin and the nation. In 1970, 87 percent of all congressional incumbents retained their seats, and 86 percent of the House seats were won comfortably, with 55 percent or more of the vote. Similarly, in Wisconsin nine of ten incumbents were re-elected, and eight of the ten House seats were won with at least 55 percent of the vote.

In summary, at the outset of the 1970 campaign, Wisconsin campaigners were faced not only with two-party competition and population factors typical of two-party states, but also with a widespread distrust for strong party organization as well as an influential number of independent voters. Various issues discussed by campaigners in other states were also utilized by the Wisconsinites.

In spite of the similarities existing between Wisconsin and other two-party states, however, this study is limited in two ways: it describes campaigners in only one state at one point in time, and it relies on a relatively small number of campaigners who were interviewed. These factors affected the techniques used to analyze the data. For example, tests of significance such as chi-square, normally applied to a sample, were not used because the study involves a population—the total number of persons running for Congress or state office under a major party label in the state of Wisconsin. The direction and strength of relationships were tested by a measure of association—Goodman-Kruskal's gamma (see the appendix for more detailed information). The small size of the population also made the use of multivariate statistical controls difficult. The more factors that are simultaneously held constant in an analysis in order to learn how they influence a relationship, the more likely that there will be too few cases in any one category to analyze properly (see appendix).

But these limitations are accompanied by benefits. Since the study covered only one state, the author was able to interview all the campaigners personally during the election period and to become familiar with the nuances of each campaign. Further, the small number of respondents is offset by the fact that a population, not a sample, of campaigners was interviewed. The campaigns studied were far from homogeneous. They included one-man staffs as well as extensive organizations; shoe-string operations as well as budgets that might be expected in a much larger state. The campaigners were interviewed in depth. The results of these interviews, with their variations in extent and style of campaigning, provide a rich source for hypotheses about campaigning and a test of many notions about campaigns, despite the limited size of the study.

In each race, interviews were sought with both the candidate and the campaign manager. The manager was not always easy to identify. The "community power" controversy of the last two decades has stimulated a concern that studies of leadership identify the real leaders—persons actually holding and exercising power—rather than simply persons whose titles indicate a potential for power. In most of the state races and those of congressional challengers, the person with the title of campaign manager was the only full-time staff member who indicated a feeling of responsibility for the rest of the staff. But the campaigns of incumbent congressmen were quite different. Most incumbents designated a prominent constituent as a figurehead manager—to avoid charges of using public funds to run their campaign—but actually relied on their administrative assistants to coordinate the campaign. In these cases the assistant was regarded as the real campaign manager unless he stated that someone else was taking primary responsibility for the organization. Out of twenty congressional and ten statewide races, with a total of 61 candidates and managers (one candidate was his own manager), 57 persons were interviewed: 28 candidates and 29 campaign managers (see the appendix for details).

The decision to interview during the campaign did not provide peaceful research conditions. But the campaign is certainly the best time to learn the campaigners' attitudes, before these attitudes are reinterpreted as a result of later experience. Since the events of the campaign are closely involved with the feelings and self-perceptions of the politician, recollections of reactions, thoughts, and even facts are likely to emerge in altered form—as the campaigner looks back—to protect or enhance his self-image in light of the election outcome. Studies of campaigning that are carried out after election day must face this risk. In fact, one of John Kingdon's most striking findings is that winning or losing has a strong effect on the candidate's perceptions of his campaign.[41] In the hope of gathering respondents' reactions—and their reinterpreted views—after they had time to reflect on the election, each respondent was sent a written questionnaire after election day (also described in the appendix).

In the next four chapters, each of the factors that have been suggested as having an influence on campaigners' behavior will be examined. And in particular, as these influences are clarified, one major difference among campaigners will be emphasized: the clear difference in temperament, political orientation, and activities between the candidates and their presumed alter-egos, the campaign managers.

2 How Uncertainty Affects Campaign Decision-Making

The suspense of a campaign and the excitement of election night stem from the uncertainty of the election outcome. That outcome can be seen as meaning life or death for certain policies or political futures. But as long as both parties have a shot at victory, the outcome remains in question until all the votes are counted.

The importance of electoral uncertainty is that when parties must compete, each must use all available resources to attract voters to its side. These resources include the personalities of the party's candidates, the tone and style of its campaign, good advertising, effective organization, dominance in party identification, and the responsiveness of its policies to public wants and needs. This last resource is the desired goal of party competition in a democracy. The uncertainty of elections serves as a potential guarantee that this resource will be used. When a candidate has viable competition, he must seriously consider the possibility that failing to use any available resource may lead to defeat.

In short, maintaining uncertainty is one method of keeping political leaders responsive to their followers. Perhaps this is what Lord Bryce was suggesting when he wrote:

In the States the principle of Popular Sovereignty is carried out (*a*) by entrusting as many offices as possible, even (in most States) judgeships, to direct popular election, so that the official may feel himself immediately responsible to the people, holding office by no pleasure but theirs; (*b*) by making terms of office short, in order that he may not forget his dependence, but shall, if he desires a renewal of his commission, be required to seek it afresh.[1]

Two other political scientists have suggested that "one of the principal arguments in favor of democratic government is that the citizen can, through periodic elections, hold his leaders responsible for their policy decisions."[2]

But does he? To maintain responsiveness it is not enough to force leaders to compete for office against one another. The voters must also be vigilant enough at election time to ferret out officials who are not being responsive to the public. But voters are not always vigilant. As noted in Chapter 1, the Survey Research Center's extensive efforts have shown that there does not seem to be much issue content in most voters' choice of candidates.[3] In fact, many voters seem to feel that their impressions about the candidate's character and personality are much more important than his positions on issues, many of which the voter may not be familiar with. It is more important, these voters would argue, to have insight into a candidate's personal qualities, which are enduring, than to know his views on issues, since the substance of issues may change a great deal in a short time. This argument has merit, even though it is hard to imagine that voters can always see a campaigner's character through the screen of a political campaign. But in general, a large proportion of voters is not vigilant in holding officials responsible at election time for their policy decisions.

Let us consider a second alternative. Even if voters do not force their representatives to be responsive, responsiveness may still occur. If leaders feel, rightly or wrongly, that the voters are determined to have their views represented, then learning and expressing public opinion may be seen as the road to public approval and re-election. This alternative rests on the plausibility of the idea that leaders feel voters are issue-oriented, even though we know most voters are not.

Evidence indicates, however, that most leaders do not believe the public is very concerned with issues. When Wisconsin candidates were asked by John Kingdon which factors were all-important to their constituents, the largest group (74 percent) cited the personal characteristics of the candidate. More than half (61 percent) felt party label was all-important, but only 34 percent cited the issues of the election. Further, while 15 percent of the candidates considered voters to be very well-informed, fully 51 percent felt that voters were not well-informed about politics.[4] Looking at the same question, Donald Stokes and Warren Miller found that while 46 percent of the congressmen they interviewed considered national issues to be quite important in enhancing their re-election and the same proportion made that judgment about traditional party loyalties, fully 85 percent felt that their personal standing was quite important for re-election.[5]

After election day campaigners in the present study were asked what determined the election results (with multiple answers permitted). The same pattern emerges. The largest group, 69 percent, chose the candidate's image; 33 percent mentioned the issues of the campaign and 26 percent cited the candidate's party label. These findings support the conclusion that the candidate considers his own image to be considerably more important to the voters than the issues are.

These leaders do not feel that voters are keeping an eye on leaders' issue positions. Are we then left to assume that candidates will be responsive to the public when they feel like it, or when they are so disposed by personality? One possible sanction on leaders remains: although they do not feel that reflecting popular opinion on all issues is necessary for re-election, they still cannot be sure what *is* necessary for re-election. Split-ticket voting has increased and party coalitions do shift. Unpredictable events occur in campaigns. And there is evidence that office-holders feel that elections can be won or lost by the decisions of a small number of voters, who may well be concerned with the responsiveness of their leaders.[6] Therefore, it is proposed, leaders may remain at least minimally sensitive to voters' concerns on the chance that some voters, perhaps enough to put them over the top, will be influenced.

Uncertainty about the election result or about the best way to win is not felt by all campaigners, however. It is a variable. To find out whether uncertainty can keep leaders responsive to public opinion, we must first learn whether they actually are uncertain. If a campaigner feels certain that he will win (or lose), the influence of uncertainty is an academic question; it will not affect his campaigning.

Campaigners were asked, "Are you pretty sure how well you'll do when the votes are in, or are you more uncertain about that?" Of 56 responses to the question, 21 answered that they were pretty sure about the results. In short, a sizable number of the Wisconsin campaigners were *not* affected by uncertainty in their campaigns. Most of these assured persons were the incumbents or their managers. (The gamma association between certainty about the election result and incumbency is .57 for candidates and .88 for managers.) The experience of winning previous elections seems to give them security. As noted above, the oddsmakers would agree that the incumbents' confidence in being re-elected is justified by past performance.

But what about campaigners who *are* uncertain about the election result? Do they tend to be more interested in and responsive to voters' opinions than the assured campaigners are? As one measure of responsiveness, campaigners were asked how they went about learning voters' views on the major issues of the campaign. The respondents were then classified according to whether or not they used *any* method of learning those views (including polls, canvassing, media reports, mail, or talking to voters). Table 2-1 shows that uncertain managers (and, to a lesser extent, candidates) *were* more likely to seek voters' opinions during the campaign. This was even true of most uncertain incumbents.

In spite of the finding that nearly 40 percent of the campaigners felt the election does not hold much suspense, uncertainty does lead to greater responsiveness in the others, and particularly the managers. Uncertain campaigners were also much more likely to include public opinion polls in their budget.

Table 2-1
Seeking Voters' Opinions and Uncertainty about the Election Result

Effort to Learn Voters' Opinions	Candidates		Managers	
	Sure	Uncertain	Sure	Uncertain
Does make an effort	62%	68%	31%	75%
Does not make an effort	38	32	69	25
	100%	100%	100%	100%
	N = 8	19	13	16

Note: Goodman-Kruskal's gamma is −.13 for candidates, −.74 for managers.

And uncertainty seems to have heightened campaigners' attention to other groups. Respondents were asked whether contributors gave money to their campaign because of a concern with issues or simply because they trusted the candidate. Uncertain campaigners were much more likely to see contributions as indications of issue preference rather than personal votes of confidence. (Gamma associations between uncertainty and the use of polls are 1.00 for candidates and .50 for managers; between uncertainty and contributors' reasons for giving to the campaign, .42 for candidates and .48 for managers.)

Two interesting conclusions can be drawn from these findings. First, uncertainty about the election result does stimulate campaigners to seek out public opinion, both from voters and contributors. This does not guarantee that these campaigners will actually reflect public opinion on particular issues. But it does indicate that one form of responsiveness—open channels of communication between leaders and followers—is enhanced by uncertainty. On the other hand, this relationship does not apply to a large number of campaigners, who tend to be incumbents. The challengers are kept responsive by uncertainty but they are likely to lose. And ironically, the managers tend to be more influenced by this stimulus for responsiveness than the candidates are. Those who are likely to win the representative positions tend to be least affected by the uncertainty that might guarantee their responsiveness. Certainly this is not what most theorists had in mind. The findings raise questions: If incumbents are not as active as challengers in learning public views during the campaign, are they much more active during their term of office? Do elected officials hear as broad a spectrum of views as campaigners do? What role do challengers and managers play in the representation of public opinion?

The fact that incumbents do not put as much effort as challengers into learning public opinion during the campaign does not seem to keep voters from re-electing those incumbents. The symbolism that surrounds elections, as well as the excitement and amusement, may be more important to voters. As Murray Edelman points out:

. . . [elections] give people a chance to express discontents and enthusiasms, to enjoy a sense of involvement. This is participation in a ritual act, however; only in a minor degree is it participation in policy formation. Like all ritual, whether in primitive or modern societies, elections draw attention to common social ties and to the importance and apparent reasonableness of accepting the public policies that are adopted. Without some such device no polity can survive and retain the support or acquiescence of its members. The key point is, however, that elections could not serve this vital social function if the common belief in direct popular control over governmental policy through elections were to be widely questioned.[7]

But different responses to uncertainty are important in the shaping of a campaign organization. Both the differences found between incumbents and challengers and between candidates and managers are a preview of the patterns to be explored in this study. One effect of uncertainty, in short, is whether or not the campaigner feels the need to seek out public opinion on issues. Other effects remain to be examined. Let us begin with three hypotheses about uncertainty, starting with the most obvious and then ranging into muddier waters.

First Hypothesis: Campaigners Who Are More Uncertain Are Likely to Work Harder in the Campaign

It has been proposed that when candidates are uncertain they will use all available resources in their drive to win. Charles O. Jones points out:

No candidate who has opposition can ever be certain which is the best campaign technique. The winners are the experts, but even they cannot afford to be confident about why they won. Analysis of almost any campaign effort will show that the candidate relies on the shotgun rather than the rifle. He wants votes on Election Day. Because there is no guaranteed appeal, the candidate relies on as many appeals as he can think of and afford.[8]

If this is the case, again uncertainty would encourage democratic practices. An uncertain campaigner would increase his communication with the voters, which might give voters a better look at the candidate's qualities.

Campaigners in Wisconsin were asked about their use of seven different methods: television, radio, newspaper advertising, campaign literature and direct mail, collateral material (buttons, bumperstickers and signs), canvassing, and personal appearances by the candidate. The evidence, reported in Table 2-2, shows that uncertain campaigners clearly use more campaign methods than the assured competitors do.

Because of the strong relationship between certainty and incumbency, these

Table 2-2
Number of Methods Used and Uncertainty about the Election Result

Number of Methods Used	Candidates		Managers	
	Sure	Uncertain	Sure	Uncertain
Six or more methods	25%	84%	46%	75%
Fewer than six methods	75	16	54	25
	100%	100%	100%	100%
	N = 8	19	13	16

Note: Gamma is $-.88$ for candidates, $-.56$ for managers.

results were recomputed to see whether incumbency rather than assurance might account for the data in Table 2-2. Among candidates it was found that incumbency did account for part of the relationship, though not all of it. Incumbency did not account for the responses of managers. Uncertainty has an independent influence on the number of methods used. Further, uncertain campaigners tend to use each method to a greater extent, as shown in Table 2-3.

One campaigner explains why uncertainty leads him to expand his campaign activities:

If somebody would come in and say, "Hey, we've got the final campaign answer and that would be radio spots at 6 a.m. and you don't have to do anything else". . . . Nobody has the courage to go along that route because it's never been tried and proven before. So a guy will decide maybe he'll run the 6 a.m. radio spots, but he'll also put up some billboards and go around shaking hands. So he wins—and it could be one of those few things or it could be the fact that his opponent was a jerk.

Another campaigner suggests:

My friend said . . . that campaigning is a little like taking mudballs and throwing them against the barn wall, like he used to do when he was a kid, at the target. You make a series of circles on the wall and pick up the mudballs. He said one out of every ten would stick, but you never knew which one, so you had to throw all ten. That's a little like politics. You've got to put some billboards up and you've got to go door-to-door, and you got to have a lot of television. . . .

The campaigners' answers indicate that another kind of uncertainty might also be prodding them to increase their use of various methods: uncertainty about the effectiveness of the techniques they are using. Some use as many methods as possible, as the campaigner stated above, in the hope that one will "stick." Others may do so because they need the reassurance that they are covering the district. For example, one manager was asked whether there was any item in his campaign budget that might not bring in any votes. He agreed and explained:

Table 2-3
Gamma Associations Between Uncertainty and Extent of Method Use

Campaign Method Used	Candidates	Managers
Television	.25	.51
Canvassing by volunteers	.43	.67
Public opinion polling	1.00	.50
Total campaign spending	.53	.57

Note: Positive gammas indicate that uncertain campaigners use more of the methods than assured campaigners do.

Oh, maybe the number of bumperstickers we've bought or the number of signs. But bumperstickers and signs are one of the few material examples of the candidacy itself, of what's happening, of what kind of support you have. So it's fun to see a lot of bumperstickers around. It's heartening. . . . At times when you're ready to do it all in, chuck it all, you see a bumpersticker, you see a sign on someone's lawn, and you think, "Hell, it can't be all that bad."

In short, uncertainty takes two forms. One involves the end result of the election. The other has to do with the means to that end, the effectiveness of techniques used to influence the election result. This second type of uncertainty was measured by asking: "Do you have a very good idea which campaign expenditures help you to win the election and which ones may not?" and classifying the responses in four categories from "very sure" to "very uncertain." This form of uncertainty will be termed method-uncertainty, in contrast to result-uncertainty.

Method-uncertainty does not affect the campaigner's use of different techniques in the same way that result-uncertainty does. The two types of uncertainty have very different consequences for candidates and managers. Among candidates, uncertainty about methods (like result-uncertainty) is strongly associated with the use of more campaign techniques. Method-uncertain candidates are also likely to spend more on their campaigns than assured candidates are. Finally, candidates uncertain about the effectiveness of various methods are quite likely to be uncertain about the election outcome as well. (Gammas relating method-uncertainty among candidates and the number of methods used, campaign spending, and result-uncertainty are .70, .45 and .60, respectively.) For candidates, uncertainty about the campaign tends to be generalized. It affects their feelings about both the outcome and the means to achieve it. And following Jones' description, it leads them to increase their efforts, relying on the shotgun rather than the rifle to keep their chances alive.

Managers respond quite differently. Those who are uncertain about method-effectiveness are also likely to be *assured* about the election result. They seem to believe that the result of the campaigning is predictable even though the cause is undetermined. And their certainty or uncertainty about the election result seems to overshadow their feelings about method-effectiveness. For example, uncertainty about method-effectiveness does not lead them to campaign harder. In fact, method-uncertain managers are slightly more likely than assured managers to *reduce* the number of methods used. They are also less likely to seek out voters' views on issues. (Gammas relating method-uncertainty among managers and the number of methods used, learning voters' views on issues, and result-uncertainty are .10, .21 and .21, respectively.) If they feel the result is assured and the means of achieving it are much less certain, perhaps these managers are reducing their use of campaign techniques, spending, and information-gathering on the assumption that the use of possibly ineffective methods is not worth their cost.

These results provide some insight into the differences between candidates' and managers' viewpoints. Candidates tend to be either completely assured or completely uncertain. If they are uncertain they are likely to require the reassurance—in the form of more methods used and more money spent—that everything possible is being done in their behalf. As Chapter 3 will show, this need for reassurance stems from the fact that candidates are more ego-involved in their campaigns than managers are. The managers, in contrast, are likely to respond pragmatically. They tend to increase the use of campaign methods only when the effectiveness of those methods is felt to be understood. The same forms of uncertainty affect candidates and managers differently.

The concept of uncertainty, in short, is more complex than has often been assumed. In particular, the two types of uncertainty differ in their relationship to information-gathering. Campaigners who are result-uncertain tend to seek out voters' feelings on issues, and the uncertain managers say they are seeking information about the opponent's campaign plans in order to better plan their own campaign. But while result-uncertainty encourages the gathering of information, *method*-uncertainty is associated with less information-seeking about voters' opinions. This holds true for both candidates and managers. Further, method-uncertain managers tend to use less reliable methods of learning voters' views—such as intuition—than do assured managers.

Another major difference, closely linked with the first, involves incumbency. While incumbents are much more likely than challengers to be *result*-assured, the challengers are significantly more likely to be assured about the effectiveness of different campaign methods. (Gamma associations between result-certainty and incumbency are .57 for candidates, .88 for managers; between method-uncertainty and incumbency, .41 for candidates and .32 for managers.) This finding contradicts David Leuthold's contention that "incumbents appeared to have a much better idea than nonincumbents about which expenditures fell into the wasted half, and incumbents were thus less likely to spend for unprofitable items."[9] It is understandable that incumbents are more assured about the outcome, but why are they less certain about which methods are best? Many incumbents stated that as they gained experience in politics they became more confident about predicting the election results but less sure why those results occurred. Challengers, with less political experience than incumbents, have not yet had their theories about method-effectiveness shattered by extensive campaigning.

One final test will be made to trace the differences between method-uncertainty and result-uncertainty. Do these two types act as blunt instruments, leading campaigners to work harder or less hard in every area, or are efforts affected only in certain areas of campaigning? Perhaps the best way to ask the question is: Which areas of campaigning tend to be expanded or contracted as the campaigner becomes more assured? Two competing ideas will be suggested. First, as the campaigner gains assurance, he becomes more removed from the campaign. He uses fewer personal appearances, shows less interest in voter and contributor opinions, and puts his efforts primarily into the media. Second, the assured campaigner cuts down on the use of the scarcest resource—money. He uses less of the expensive techniques such as the media because he feels they are no longer needed for his re-election. He concentrates on the less costly methods: personal appearances, canvassing, bumperstickers, student volunteers. Table 2-4 compares the level of method use with the two types of campaign uncertainty.

The table shows that the dominant response to assurance about the election result, in nearly every case, is to cut down on method use. Result-assured managers say that they reduce their use of every technique. They report more severe cutbacks than candidates do. This again reflects the candidates' desire for a broad-gauged attack even when the outcome seems certain. The assured candidates say that they are cutting back on most face-to-face methods. They report even deeper reductions in the media, especially in radio and polling. Certainty about the election result gives campaigners the confidence to reduce their campaigning across the board, decreasing personal involvement as well as use of the more costly media.

Those who are confident about what works in campaigns, on the other hand, reduce their method use more selectively. They report retaining most of the less costly face-to-face methods—bumperstickers, canvassing and personal appearances—and cutting down on the more expensive media and polls. Again it is interesting to compare candidates and managers. Assured managers are less likely to cut back on television, radio, polls and spending, techniques closely associated with New Politics campaigning. But they report more cutbacks of the candi-

Table 2-4
Gamma Associations Between Uncertainty and Extent of Method Use (2)

Method Used	Result-Uncertainty		Method-Uncertainty	
	Candidates	Managers	Candidates	Managers
Media and spending				
Television	.25	.51	.52	.11
Radio	.81	.90	.31	−.25
Polls	1.00	.50	.37	.20
Campaign spending	.53	.57	.45	.09
Face-to-face methods				
Bumperstickers, signs	−.12	.67	−.12	−.08
Canvassing	.43	.67	−.14	−.18
Personal appearances	.10	.72	−.64	−.27
Student volunteers	.32	.45	.09	.38

Note: Positive associations indicate that the greater the certainty, the less the campaign method is used.

date's personal appearances than the candidates do. It appears that the managers consider the media to be more necessary than the candidate's personal involvement with voters. The candidates' responses, in contrast, indicate that method-assurance leads them to believe their own personal impact on voters is the key to their success.

Another factor must be considered when the relationship between uncertainty and campaign effort is discussed: the influence of incumbency. It was found that result-assured *candidates* were more likely to cut down on campaigning if they were incumbents. Conversely, the tendency for result-assured *managers* to decrease their campaigning was stronger among challengers. In short, uncertainty has a complex influence on campaigns. It affects persons with different positions and levels of experience differently.

In summary, result-certainty acts like a blunt instrument. It produces less campaign effort on all fronts. On the other hand, a method-assured campaigner responds more selectively. Seeing some methods as especially important, he concentrates on those methods and reduces the use of others. The decision as to which methods are most important depends in part on whether it is being made by a candidate or a manager.

Second Hypothesis: Uncertainty Leads
Campaigners to Avoid Change

Uncertainty might cause a campaigner to try new ways of campaigning on the chance that they might be helpful. Or it might make a campaigner cautious, unwilling to disturb an already precarious situation by breaking with tradition. Several authors have proposed the latter idea. They state that because there is no sure knowledge about what wins votes, a wise campaigner will stick with anything that has been successful in the past. As Nelson Polsby and Aaron Wildavsky suggest: "In the absence of a special effort, in the presence of enormous uncertainties and the inevitable insecurities, the forces of tradition may do more to shape a campaign than the overt decisions of the candidates possibly can."[10] Numerous examples can be found in political science studies:

... [campaigners] normally review only those means (and goals) used before. Campaign issues, strategies, or techniques that are novel, remote, poorly understood, or whose consequences constitute sharp changes from the *status quo*, are usually avoided. Decision-making is thus concentrated within the most well-explored areas of the political world.[11]

Charles Clapp, on the other hand, writes that uncertainty should lead to innovations in campaigning: "Waging an effective campaign is, understandably, a major concern of congressmen, and they are constantly searching for new techniques. .... Politicians seldom take elections for granted, and many are constantly seeking new means by which to strengthen their hold on their constituency."[12] If campaigners are thought to be tradition-minded by some authors and innovative by others, perhaps the effects of uncertainty or assurance may help explain when campaigners accept change and when they do not. What is the relationship between certainty-uncertainty and traditionalism or innovation in political campaigns?

Several questions asked in this study deal with the campaigner's willingness to make changes. One question measures a general attitude toward innovation: "Do you think a candidate should stick pretty closely to the strategy he planned before the campaign started, or should he be very flexible and respond to events as they happen?" Two other items are also attitudinal but refer specifically to the 1970 campaign: whether the respondent would consider making changes in the present campaign while it was going on, and (asked after the election) in retrospect, whether he would like to have made changes in the campaign. Two more items involve reports of behavior: whether the respondent is using the same methods as in his last campaign (or, for first-timers, "tried and true" methods), and whether most of his campaign workers have been associated with his previous campaign. The latter applies to many challengers as well as incumbents since several challengers had assembled staffs in previous campaigns for other offices.

Table 2-5 presents a matrix of these five measures to see whether they are different ways of asking the same question or whether they tap different elements of the willingness to accept change. Some interesting findings can be seen in these data. Starting with the measures that involve reported behavior— labeled "uses same methods" and "worker turnover"—there is a marked difference between candidates and managers. Managers' responses to the behavioral measures were very consistent. Those who used new campaign methods were very likely also to have chosen a new staff. Among candidates the two behavioral measures were only weakly related.

Associations among the three attitudinal measures show the opposite results. The attitudes of the candidates were very strongly interrelated. Those who believed that change is generally good also expressed willingness to accept change in this specific campaign, while it was going on and in retrospect. On the other hand, managers' general attitudes toward change were only slightly related to their willingness to make changes in the 1970 campaign. Among both candidates and managers, however, the attitudinal measures were very weakly related to behavior regarding change. In fact, among candidates there was a negative relationship between attitudes and behavior.

These results help show the differences between candidates and managers. Candidates tend to express more consistent *attitudes* toward change than managers do, but these attitudes do not produce consistent behavior regarding changes in the campaign. Managers, on the other hand, are very consistent in

Table 2-5
Gamma Matrix of Five Measures of Willingness to Accept Change

	Candidates			
	Same Methods	Worker Turnover	Make any Changes	Change in Retrospect
Uses same methods	–			
Worker turnover	.14	–		
Make any changes	–.02	–.37	–	
Change in retrospect	.29	–.23	.48	–
Flexibility	–.08	.00	.65	.53

	Managers			
	Same Methods	Worker Turnover	Make any Changes	Change in Retrospect
Uses same methods	–			
Worker turnover	.85	–		
Make any changes	.06	.01	–	
Change in retrospect	.02	.14	.22	–
Flexibility	–.22	.19	.10	.12

Note: Positive gammas indicate a positive relationship among measures of willingness to change.

their behavior involving change. The managers seem to place a higher value on consistency in their actual decisions than the candidates do. This might indicate that managers approach campaign changes in a more pragmatic way than candidates do.

Looking now at the relationship between willingness to change and result-uncertainty, the findings belie the idea that uncertainty leads to traditionalism. In general, uncertainty is related to acceptance of change, not avoidance of it. Result-uncertain campaigners were more likely to try new campaign methods, to have more worker turnover and to accept flexibility in general. (Gamma associations between result-uncertainty and use of the same methods are .33 for candidates, .41 for managers; with worker turnover, .33 for candidates, .78 for managers; with flexibility, .20 for candidates, .14 for managers.) The assured campaigners were the traditionalists. Here are reasons offered by two result-assured campaigners:

I'm using the same approaches [as in the last election]. They've been tested and tried, and I think the prize is too valuable—when you've been *successful* at it—to deviate from the idea and the principle of getting it. So since it's been tested and tried, and worked in the past, I choose to do it until I find that the vote is slipping, and then I'll look to other means.

The exasperated manager of a long-time incumbent describes his boss:

No, he doesn't change easily. He's got—look at this [a matchbook cover with the candidate's name on a banner]. That damn blue scroll. His first campaign had this [in the 1930s] and how *hard* I've tried to change it. This is my third time around with his campaigns, and I've made some changes, modernized some of the styles of the materials, but this thing he clings to just so desperately—his reasoning being that it's an identification which has become like a trademark. And so he doesn't change very readily—it's like pulling whale teeth to get him to change.

These result-assured campaigners show a decidedly unassured preference for traditional methods of campaigning. Comments by assured respondents indicate that they fear change because they dislike the unpredictable and because they identify with methods that have been a part of previous winning campaigns.

But before drawing conclusions, let us look at the other measure of uncertainty, having to do with method-effectiveness. Here again, although the results are less clear-cut, a contrasting view is presented. In general, method-uncertain campaigners tend to avoid changes in the campaign.

In summary, campaigners assured about the election result tend to be traditional in their approach: they avoid changes in their campaigns. Those who are method-assured are somewhat more willing to make changes, at least in terms of their reported attitudes toward the 1970 campaign. These two conclusions appear to conflict. But the pattern becomes clearer when incumbency is taken into account.

Incumbents were much less willing to accept change than challengers were. Again, this was especially true of the incumbents' reported behavior and attitudes toward the 1970 campaign.[a] Further, incumbents were more assured about the election result yet less assured about method-effectiveness than were challengers. And both of these characteristics—result-certainty and method-*uncertainty*—were also related to an unwillingness to accept change. When incumbency was held constant in the relationships between uncertainty and change, those relationships diminished. The fear of change, then, is due largely to the effects of incumbency on the campaigners.

The tendency for incumbents to avoid change may be self-reinforcing. Perhaps the use of traditional methods in campaigning proves so successful that the traditional campaigner becomes an incumbent and keeps using his tested methods. Or it may be that incumbents, who have a striking tendency to win

[a]Gammas are as follows:

Incumbency x	Candidates	Managers
Use of same methods	.83	.60
Worker turnover	.42	.65
Make changes during campaign	.47	.55
Make changes in retrospect	.55	.73
Flexibility	.22	.27

elections, prefer to stick with tradition for other reasons, perhaps because they feel secure with methods that have brought victory in the past.

This self-fulfilling prophecy connecting winning and traditionalism can be examined empirically. First it can be tested whether the experience of winning is associated with a desire to avoid changes in future campaigns. When the Wisconsin campaigners were asked after the election whether they would have liked to use more of each campaign method (presuming the funds were available), the winners tended to say that they would *not* have conducted a broader campaign even if money had been no object. This was especially true of candidates. Managers, interestingly enough, were not as reluctant to expand the campaign. The losers were more likely to report that if they had the campaign to do over again, they would have made changes in its operation and organization and (among candidates) would expand their use of various campaign techniques. (Gammas relating the use of more campaign methods to the election result are .68 for candidates, .02 for managers; relating willingness to change (in retrospect) to the election result, .73 for candidates, .79 for managers.)

It seems obvious that someone who fails is likely to wish he had done things differently. But it is also true that keeping the same methods (or traditional methods) from year to year appears to result in electoral success. Table 2-6 compares the election results of those who innovated in campaign methods and those who did not. When incumbency was held constant, those challengers who used traditional methods of campaigning were still more likely to win than were challengers who made innovations. In fact, this small number of winning challengers was even more likely to have used traditional methods than were the winning incumbents. Again, this was more true of candidates than of managers, suggesting that the winning managers are more willing to take risks with new approaches than are the more personally-involved candidates.

Table 2-6
Use of the Same Methods as in Last Campaign and the 1970 Election Result[a]

| | Candidates | | Managers | |
Use of Same Methods[b]	Won	Lost	Won	Lost
Did use same methods	75%	25%	58%	50%
Made changes in degree only	25	38	17	12
Made major changes	0	38	25	38
	100%	101%	100%	100%
N =	12	8	12	8

[a]Gamma is .83 for candidates, .19 for managers.

[b]The difference in responses between candidates and managers who worked in the same campaigns is explained by the fact that campaigners' perceptions, rather than some objective measure of innovation, are being explored, and these perceptions did differ within campaigns.

Other forms of political experience were also related to traditionalism. For example, managers who had run a campaign before were less willing to accept changes. This was especially true of the managers' reported behavior and less true of their attitudes toward change. Again, experience led managers to consistently avoid change in behavior but did not cause them to develop inflexible attitudes. Similarly, the campaigner's success or failure in previous elections had some effect on his attitude toward change. On most questions, candidates who had previously won office were least willing to accept change. Candidates who had previously run unsuccessfully, on the other hand, were most accepting of change. This does not mean that the impact of experience or incumbency completely explains the relationship between uncertainty and willingness to change, however. Uncertainty does have an independent influence.

In summary, experience at successful campaigning is usually associated with certainty about the election results and a reluctance to make changes in the campaign. Incumbents, it has been determined, tend to do very little innovating in campaigns. Incumbents tend to be re-elected. And campaigners are more likely to be re-elected if they keep using traditional methods. Innovation in campaigning can only be expected from the challengers, who do any innovating at some risk to their already-slim prospects of winning. So the traditionalism of winning campaigns is maintained over time. This portion of the democratic system does not reward the input of new ideas—at least as these campaigners saw it. Thus, the successful campaign reflects the tendency of any institution to grow into tested patterns of activity.

Third Hypothesis: The Campaign Organization Has Limited Tolerance for Uncertainty

Many students of organizational behavior have concluded that organizations typically try to predict and control as much as possible about the forces that affect them. Anthony Downs has stated that "coping with uncertainty is a major function of nearly every significant institution in society; therefore it shapes the nature of each."[13] As two students of complex organizations—Richard Cyert and James March—propose:

> ... organizations avoid uncertainty: (1) They avoid the requirement that they correctly anticipate events in the distant future by using decision rules emphasizing short-run reaction to short-run feedback rather than anticipation of long-run uncertain events. ... (2) They avoid the requirement that they anticipate future reactions of other parts of their environment by arranging a negotiated environment. They impose plans, standard operating procedures. ... In short, they achieve a reasonably manageable decision situation by avoiding planning where plans depend on predictions of uncertain future events ...[14]

Since campaigns and other organizations have uncertainty in common, we would expect campaigners to regard uncertainty as a negative force to be controlled as much as possible, and to find campaigners focussing on short-range decision-making, as Cyert and March suggest.

Some support for the first part of this description is found in the managers' attitudes toward the candidates. To keep the campaign under control, the manager must be able to control his own uncertainty about the candidate's activities and independence. The actions of the candidate are a part of the uncertain environment the manager must deal with. In the interview managers were asked, "Given the personality of the candidate, what kinds of campaign activities do you think he's best suited for, and what kinds would you urge him to avoid?" The answers were divided into four categories according to the manager's expressed enthusiasm for directing the candidate's actions. Nearly 40 percent of the uncertain managers expressed strong enthusiasm for directing the candidate. None said that he would not attempt to channel the candidate's activities. On the other hand, only 25 percent of the result-assured managers stated that they tried to control their candidate, and another quarter refused to direct his activities at all. Uncertain managers attempted to control their uncertainty, at least as far as their candidates' actions are concerned.

But further data show that this desire for control, as a response to campaign uncertainty, is more likely to be applied to long-range planning rather than short-range activities. These responses do not follow the pattern described by Cyert and March in this respect. Candidates and managers were asked: "How much of the time you spend on the campaign is spent in (long-run) strategy-planning, as opposed to going out and campaigning?" Result-uncertain campaigners were more likely than result-assured campaigners to say that they spent half or more of their time in long-range planning. This response was chosen by 18 percent of the uncertain candidates but none of the assured candidates, and by 53 percent of the uncertain managers, compared with 36 percent of the assured managers. When campaigners feel uncertain about the results of their energies, they often try to adapt by making plans for the future in spite of the considerable uncertainty involved in doing so.

But in contrast to other kinds of organizations, these campaigners also accepted uncertainty to a great extent. As John Kingdon has suggested, many campaigners feel that uncertainty serves a positive function for the campaign.[15] When asked: "Do you think that it's *good* for a campaigner to be worried about whether he's going to win?" 41 of the 57 respondents in this study agreed. Three campaigners were alone in considering uncertainty a bad thing. The remaining persons questioned the wording of the item, indicating that worry is a destructive emotion but that a campaigner must be *concerned*. One incumbent candidate mentioned:

On the tail end of a campaign in particular, you get tired, and you get not only physically tired, but you get mentally and emotionally exhausted. It's awfully easy to say, "Oh, to heck with it. I'm going to forget about it for the night and just go out and have dinner and go home and read a book and forget about this thing." So it's easy to do that. And when you're really fagged out—so I think probably the spur of uncertainty does keep the individual candidate going—because human nature is such that when you get exhausted you just want to quit.

A challenger said:

I worry about everything. I'm a compulsive worrier, which is good because I work harder. I worry about whether we're doing a good job. But to worry compulsively to the point that you're constantly pacing the floor, then no, because you're not out shaking hands. Every time I get worried so that I forget to go out to the plant gates, then I know I'm worrying too much.

These comments suggest the reason why uncertainty is tolerated by many campaigners. It helps to motivate them by throwing a little fear into their hearts at times when they feel like relaxing a little.

Incumbents as well as challengers said that uncertainty is good for a campaigner. Their comments often included admonitions about the dangers of overconfidence. Some specifically stated that an overconfident campaigner will not be a good public servant because he will not pay enough attention to the voters' ideas. Many others spoke more pragmatically, warning that once a campaigner has lost his lean and hungry look, he may risk defeat at the hands of a harder-working candidate. Even those campaigners who confidently expected to win or lose still paid their respects to the power of uncertainty.

But the effects of result-uncertainty on the behavior of incumbents are limited. Uncertainty about the election result can stimulate campaigners to innovate, to use more campaign methods and to gather more information about voters. Most incumbents, however, are not result-uncertain. Does this mean that incumbents are only paying lip-service to the value of uncertainty, or does uncertainty condition their actions in some way? Perhaps the best way to understand the effect of uncertainty on incumbents is to imagine what might happen if incumbents *were* overconfident. Although the oversized winning margins of some congressmen might suggest that they could win without even conducting a campaign, every incumbent used at least a minimal number of campaign methods. The Wisconsin incumbent who ran the least active campaign saw his usually thundering margin of victory reduced to 52 percent. Even though they feel they will win under normal conditions, incumbents still recognize the value of uncertainty in keeping them working.

Therefore, just as campaigners seem to accept the need for competition, they accept the usefulness of uncertainty because it serves a purpose for them. The ability to accept uncertainty even when the stakes are very high may help explain why political personalities do not always respond like participants in other types of organizations. Political groups, as a result of their commitment to democratic symbols, are forced to forego some of the reassurance provided by efforts to control their environment in order to maintain the belief—if not the reality—of free competition for public office. This symbolism, if it can produce voluntary restraint in a situation fraught with conflict, must be a very powerful force.

Other students of psychology have pointed out the nature of the restraint that sets political organizations apart from other groups. Harold Lasswell in his landmark work *Psychopathology and Politics* states that "the political man is the one whose principal value is the pursuit of power,"[16] yet that political man characteristically rationalizes his use of politics in terms of the public interest. Robert Lane helps to explain this process by suggesting that persons with a moderate desire for power over others are more likely to seek an outlet in politics than are people with strong power needs. He cites studies indicating that highly power-oriented individuals are less likely to become involved in campaigning than other people are. The need for a politician to relate effectively to other people, the fact that much political work is mundane rather than glory-filled, make it more likely that "in adult life the search for the jugular of power may very likely lead to the world of finance, journalism, or industry instead of politics."[17]

Persons who are attracted to political activity, then, do pay their respects to the rules of competition, including an acceptance of uncertainty that might be considered very unusual in a more tightly controlled and directed political system. The activities of candidates' "dirty tricks squads" have recently received national attention. It is interesting to ponder, however, that given the strong temptation to "influence" election results, most candidates feel they must restrain their impulses to do so (whether because of their belief in democracy or because of their fear of getting caught).

Summary and Conclusions

A sense of uncertainty about the election result has a strong and important impact on the process of campaigning. Uncertainty acts as a positive force for democracy, keeping the uncertain campaigners open to new ideas and responsive to the public. The problem, however, is that only slightly more than half of the Wisconsin respondents were actually uncertain about the election result. These uncertain campaigners tended to be challengers rather than incumbents and were less likely to be winners in the election. These findings give cause for concern. They show that incumbents tend to put less effort into their campaigns and also tend to cling to traditional campaign practices. If winners are those who do put the least effort into seeking office and are the most reluctant to break with tested methods, what effect does this have on the political system? Is the campaign's primary function simply to validate and entrench the existing leadership? Does traditionalism in campaigning have any relationship to a desire for traditionalism in governmental policy as well? These questions require further study. It is clear, however, that while uncertainty in political competition does serve a democratic function, its effect is minimal on those politicians who will actually take office after election day. Uncertainty reminds incumbents to campaign, but uncertainty alone does not guarantee that they will respond to public opinion.

This chapter has also begun to trace differences between candidates and managers—differences that will become more patterned and more pronounced in the next three chapters. The most striking findings are these:

Uncertainty has a stronger effect on managers than on candidates. Uncertain managers express greater eagerness to learn voters' views than uncertain candidates do. And uncertainty leads managers to increase their use of various campaign methods more than it does candidates. This implies that managers respond more pragmatically to uncertainty than candidates do. When managers are uncertain about the election result, they tend to expand their campaign efforts as insurance against defeat; in contrast, when they feel assured, they feel free to decrease their campaigning.

Candidates' responses to result-uncertainty are not as clear cut. Uncertain candidates do not increase their efforts as much as managers do, but on the other hand, assured candidates are not as willing to give up campaign methods as assured managers are. A particular source of difference is the candidate's own activity in the campaign. Managers who are assured about the election results are willing to sharply reduce the use of canvassing and the number of personal appearances by the candidate. This is not the case with candidates. Even when assured, they are unlikely to cut down on their personal appearances. In fact, candidates assured about method-effectiveness tend to *increase* their personal appearances, evidently in the belief that their personal effectiveness is one of the campaign's best assets. The managers are not as convinced, perhaps out of a desire to keep the candidate from overworking, or perhaps because they have a more realistic view about the numbers of voters actually reached and influenced by personal appearances.

In short, candidates and managers who feel assured about method-effectiveness tend to have greatest confidence in the methods linked with their own activities. Although method-assurance permits all campaigners to reduce the use of some methods, candidates do not reduce their use of personal appearances, canvassing by volunteers, or the collateral material—bumperstickers and buttons—that candidates often distribute when visiting areas where constituents gather; managers are not likely to reduce their use of television and radio, or a large campaign budget.

How can particular methods be linked with candidates rather than managers, or *vice versa*? The link between candidates and face-to-face methods is easy to understand. The candidate, as later chapters will show, is the campaign's emissary to the voters. He probably has a facility for meeting large numbers of people. He probably feels more comfortable concentrating on personal appearances, which usually provide him with the recognition accorded a person of note, rather than on radio and newspaper advertisements that do not provide such personal recognition. The manager, on the other hand, is not likely to be recognized by crowds. He has chosen to work with a staff of political activists, and it seems reasonable to expect that he is more apt to be inclined toward organizational activity than toward meeting voters and "pressing the flesh."

For example, result-uncertain managers tend to concentrate on long-range planning much more than uncertain candidates do. Candidates, whether uncertain or assured, are more likely to say they spend most of their time going out and campaigning, not planning. Managers are more involved in staff activities. They seem to avoid (or do not have time for) personal campaigning. Managers may show a greater affinity to the mass media and a large campaign budget for several reasons. As pragmatic campaigners, the managers may be more inclined to trust methods that reach the largest number of voters for the smallest amount of effort. This interest in efficiency has increased recently with the development of New Politics campaigning. The New Politics, involving extensive use of mass media and polling, is an attempt to apply principles of merchandising and executive management to politics. One of the most notable results of the New Politics has been the shift from candidate-led, loosely-organized campaigns to organizations tightly programmed by a trained staff. Specialists in the New Politics have rarely been candidates; more often, campaign consultants or public relations experts have brought these techniques into campaigns. Since managers are not as oriented toward personal contact with voters as candidates are, they may be less wedded to face-to-face techniques and more likely to accept the trend toward media campaigns.

It was demonstrated that managers show more consistent behavior regarding change than candidates do. It is proposed (and will be further discussed in Chapter 3) that candidates are more personally involved, more ego-involved in the campaign than managers are. Their ego-involvement intervenes between their attitudes and their behavior, strongly affecting their activities in the campaign. For example, candidates are more likely than managers to retain traditional methods but less likely to retain workers from previous campaigns. Candidates may feel psychologically attached to the methods that brought them victory, but less involved with the volunteers who have worked for them. Because of their ego-involvement, candidates' change-related behavior is not consistent at all, although they tend to have strongly interrelated *attitudes* toward innovation. Managers, on the other hand, are less ego-involved and therefore can be more pragmatic and realistic about the decisions to be made. While their attitudes are not very consistent with their behavior, their actual behavioral choices are highly consistent.

Several characteristics have been suggested, in short, to help define the position of the candidate in contrast to the position of the manager. The greater ego-involvement of candidates compared with the more pragmatic involvement of managers has consequences for the methods they rely on and the consistency of their behavior. The direction of their concerns—outward to the electorate or inward to the staff—affects the type of planning they do and the emphasis they give to different activities in the campaign. In the next chapter more attention will be given to the personality characteristics that differentiate the two positions.

3

Personalities in Campaigns: The Effects of Tolerance of Ambiguity

An observer of the 1962 Massachusetts Senate race, pitting Ted Kennedy against Eddie McCormack, noted: "McCormack does not enjoy the rigors of campaigning as much as Kennedy does; he does not meet people easily, as Kennedy does; and he is not as facile as Kennedy with the handshake, the smile, and the quick hello."[1] The observer concluded that as a result, McCormack did not devote as much time to campaigning as Kennedy did. A crucial campaign decision—the extent to which the candidate himself became personally involved in the campaign—depended in part on the personality of the campaigner.

This chapter will suggest that personality traits do have considerable impact on decisions made in the campaign. The ability of the candidate and his manager to carry out the strategy they set forth, the kinds of campaign activities on which they spend the bulk of their energies, and their feelings about voters, activists, and even each other—all these elements of the campaign are influenced by the personalities of the principal actors, the candidates and managers.

Personality is an extremely complex and fruitful area of analysis, but hard to define. In general, however, students of personality are concerned with individual differences in attitudes and psychological attributes: "the configuration of individual characteristics and ways of behaving which determines an individual's unique adjustments to his environment."[2]

As the last chapter indicated, uncertain and ambiguous situations are very much a part of the campaign environment. Candidates and managers have found many ways to adjust to campaign uncertainty. Each individual campaigner may have a characteristic approach to uncertain situations that has become a part of his personality. His general tolerance or intolerance of ambiguous situations, for example, may make him receptive to certain kinds of campaign decisions and inclined to reject others. In this chapter, the Wisconsin campaigners' tolerance of ambiguity will be measured as the first test of interaction between their personalities and their campaigning.

What We Know about Personality in Politics

Several personality traits have been thought to influence political attitudes and behavior. Investigations of these traits can be divided into two types: studies of traits that encourage a person to participate in politics and traits that affect his activities once he has begun to participate. This chapter will show that tolerance of ambiguity has effects in both categories.

41

Studies in the first category demonstrate that certain kinds of personalities are more likely to be attracted to politics than are other types of personalities. Many researchers, for example, have asked whether people recruited into political candidacy are more likely than nonpoliticians to have high self-esteem and a strong need for power. James David Barber has suggested that persons who decide to run for office are likely to have either fairly high or fairly low self-esteem compared with the rest of the population.[3] On the other hand, John B. McConaughy, in a study of South Carolina state legislators, wrote that those politicians were more self-confident than the general male population. They were much less neurotic, more self-sufficient, decidedly more extroverted, only slightly more dominant, and less irritable and tense than the average man.[4]

Two other researchers, Herbert Jacob and Rufus P. Browning, administered a projective psychological test to elected local leaders in Louisiana and an Eastern city to measure their motivation for power, achievement, and affiliation. They found that politicians scored no differently on these traits than did a matched sample of nonpoliticians. But they further found that politicians whose positions had a high potential for power and achievement were more likely to score high on these two traits than were other politicians. And in communities where politics was at the center of attention, politicians were more likely to be power- and achievement-oriented than in communities where politics commanded little interest.[5]

These studies all suggest that certain personality traits are easily adapted to political activity, and that persons with these traits are more likely to be politically involved than other persons are. The traits include extremes in self-esteem, greater self-sufficiency, and an interest in power and achievement. Later we will see whether tolerance of ambiguity is an aid or a barrier to active politicking. But looking beyond the time an individual first enters politics, do certain personality traits affect his choices, his activities, his success?

There is some evidence that personality does influence campaign behavior. A recent study traced the patterns of decision-making found in the 1964 campaigns of President Lyndon Johnson and Barry Goldwater. The contrast in the two approaches is best summarized, the authors suggest, by Theodore H. White's description of the Republican nominee: "Where his conqueror, Lyndon B. Johnson, knows there are only pressures and directions, Goldwater is a man who believes there are certainties."[6] The main reason for the difference in the two styles, the authors propose, is the difference in the personalities of the key figures involved.

In another example of the effect of personality traits on campaign decisions, Murray Levin describes another Massachusetts contender, Endicott Peabody, the 1960 Democratic candidate for governor. Peabody, Levin points out, was the underdog in the Democratic primary. But while the natural role for the underdog is to wage an aggressive campaign, an adviser suggested that Peabody and many of his braintrusters

... tended to accept as valid any information that permitted them to maintain the nonaggressive posture that suited them temperamentally. ... His [Peabody's] essential personality probably would lead him, in most situations, to select the alternative most likely to win friends and least likely to create enemies.[7]

Levin's portrayal shows a nonaggressive personality choosing a style of campaigning that in objective terms did not hold much promise of success. It provides a good example, Levin feels, of the conflict between a "rational" strategy and a candidate whose personality would not permit him to carry out that strategy.

But there is another side to the argument that personality has enough influence on campaign behavior to justify further exploration. Some political psychologists claim that the effect of personality on politics is quite limited. Herbert McClosky, studying the trait of personal conservatism, found many interesting relationships with other psychological variables. For instance, persons scoring as extreme conservatives were more likely than others to be hostile and suspicious toward other people, to be inflexible, and to demonstrate a lot of defensiveness to protect their own egos. But when he compared personal conservatism with political attitudes, McClosky found fairly low correlations.[8] In this case, personality did not have an impact on political viewpoints.

David O. Sears sums up the literature on personality and politics by stating that personality variables have not been shown to relate strongly to political or policy attitudes. Sears feels, rather, that "the most stable and meaningful political attitudes are those referring to groups, especially the political parties," and that researchers have found no clear relationship between personality traits and the choice of political parties.[9]

Interestingly, then, writers who have found a relationship between personality and politics tend to have studied political leaders or activists. Research on public opinion and mass political behavior usually discounts the importance of personality. One likely explanation is that the level of an individual's involvement determines whether or not his personality is expressed in politics. For people who have a high degree of political interest and participation, their deeper orientations may help guide their activity. For the voting public, on the other hand, political interest and concern have generally been found to be *under*whelming. Political affairs do not touch most voters deeply enough to call forth their personal mechanisms of coping with the world.

In his discussion of personality and politics, Fred I. Greenstein supports the idea that an individual's personality is more likely to be expressed in politics when he is actively participating.[10] Greenstein's aim is to clarify the conditions in which personal variability (a broad definition of personality) may have more of an impact on behavior. He discusses a number of these conditions. Greater affective or emotional involvement, he suggests, promotes the influence of personality on behavior. Affective involvement is very common in politics, as will be shown in this and other chapters. Three other conditions cited by Greenstein also bear a striking resemblance to conditions usually found in campaigns. Ambiguous situations, he says, heighten the effects of personality. Situations in which sanctions are not attached to the possible courses of action, or in which an individual tends to withstand those sanctions, are also cited. Situations without sanctions provide an individual with few guidelines for behavior. He has to make choices without knowing for sure whether those choices lead to reward or punishment. This is certainly true of campaigns. Candidates and managers constantly make decisions in the hope of reaching victory, avoiding defeat. But not all the Wisconsin campaigners were sure which campaign activities would accomplish these goals.

Greenstein also cites situations that demand a great deal of time and effort. Campaigns can vary a lot on this dimension. Some campaigners put in relatively little effort while others devote all their waking hours to the race. But in general the conditions described by Greenstein do resemble those of political campaigns. Therefore the campaign is a good setting for studying the impact of personality on politics. By examining the effects of one personality trait, it is possible to identify some of this impact.

Measuring Tolerance of Ambiguity

The campaigner's tolerance of ambiguity was measured in this study by an adaptation of a questionnaire originally developed by Stanley Budner. Budner defined the trait as the tendency to see ambiguous conditions as threatening.[11] (The test and its documentation can be found in the appendix.) This trait is very similar to the concept of rigidity. It falls within a cluster of personality traits that can be called "authoritarian."[12] These traits include conventionality, dogmatism about religious beliefs, favorable attitudes toward censorship, and intolerance. They have been the subject of a great deal of social science research during the last two decades. This is the context of tolerance of ambiguity as a personality trait. However, it is being tested here not because it relates to authoritarianism but because of its connection with the uncertainty of the campaign.

As Figure 3-1 shows, the Wisconsin campaigners tended to cluster on the tolerant side of the range of possible test scores. When the campaigners' scores are compared with those of nine samples of students tested by Budner (a comparison can be found in the appendix), the Wisconsin group's average score is similar to those of the student groups. Although data are not available on the tolerance levels of other nonstudents, it seems reasonable to assume that students would be relatively tolerant of ambiguity. Therefore the campaigners are probably more tolerant of ambiguity than the average voter is. Perhaps this tolerance made it easier for them to engage in political activity.

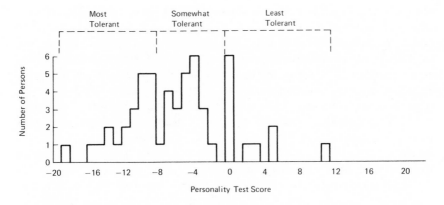

Figure 3-1. Distribution of Personality Test Scores. Note: The zero point represents the mean possible score, with the distribution divided into three clusters in relation to the mean.

Tolerance and Change

Having found that campaigners are relatively accepting of a condition that usually prevails in campaigns, it is time to look at the consequences of this personality trait. First, tolerance of ambiguity was tested against a set of campaign decisions that seem logically related: the campaigner's willingness to make changes in his campaign. Presumably a campaigner who can tolerate more ambiguity would be better able to accept changes from established practices than would the less tolerant, more rigid campaigner. Table 3-1 presents the results of this test. Willingness to change was measured by the five change-related questions introduced in the last chapter. The table shows that this personality trait does affect a cluster of attitudes and behavior in campaigning. Here is proof that personality can affect some very important decision-making by politically active people. The more tolerant campaigners are more likely to accept change. All but two associations are in the predicted direction. Controls for incumbency,

Table 3-1
Gamma Associations Between Willingness to Change and Tolerance

Measure of Willingness to Change	Candidates	Managers
Uses same methods as in last campaign	.34	.11
Worker turnover since last campaign	−.30	.71
Willing to make changes during campaign	.56	−.42
Would have made changes, in retrospect	.54	.14
Considers flexibility a good thing	.63	.26

uncertainty, and party affiliation do not change these relationships in any marked or consistent direction.

But one other factor does affect the relationships, as Table 3-1 shows. The associations are much stronger and more consistent among candidates than among managers. To explain this difference between candidates and managers, let us examine the findings somewhat differently. In the last chapter the measures of willingness to change were divided into three groups: a measure of general feelings about change, two measures of attitudes toward making changes in the 1970 campaign, and two measures of actual behavioral change in that campaign. These measures can be pictured as forming a scale ranging from deepest-held attitudes to interpersonal behavior. The personality trait can be considered the deepest-held attitude—the response most basic to the individual. Next would be ranked the general attitude about flexibility; then the specific attitudes, and finally, the reports of behavior. Applying this distinction to the data, Table 3-1 shows that among candidates tolerance of ambiguity is most strongly linked with the variable "closest" to it: the general attitude toward flexibility. Personality had less effect on feelings about the 1970 campaign, and still less to do with reported behavior, although even one of these latter relationships is significant. This is a pattern that would be expected if personality were to affect politics. Personality would have more effect on attitudes than behavior, since a person's behavior is determined by conditions in his environment as well as conditions within himself. The results are shown graphically in Figure 3-2.

This pattern was not found among managers. Tolerance of ambiguity was most strongly related to a measure of behavior: worker turnover. But this

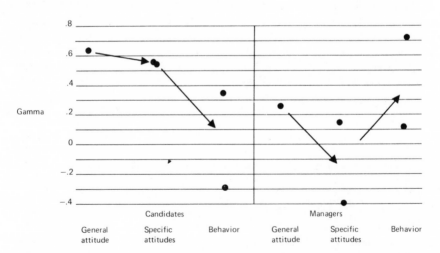

Figure 3-2. Gamma Associations Between Willingness to Change and Tolerance.

relationship was not mediated by stronger associations with any of the attitudes toward change. Among managers, tolerance of ambiguity does not consistently influence attitudes and behavior. These findings hold true even when incumbency is held constant, although the relationships between tolerance and change are usually weaker among incumbents (who tend to avoid change) than among challengers.

Why does this personality trait affect candidates differently from managers? It was suggested earlier that personality has more impact when the individual is more affectively involved in his activities. It may be that candidates and managers differ in the nature of their involvement in the campaign. It seems likely that candidates are more affectively involved than managers—involved in a personal or ego sense. Perhaps this is because of their greater visibility, and because of the candidate-centered tradition of American campaigning. Candidates are constantly on the front lines. Running for their livelihood, they are likely to put a lot of emotional energy into a campaign. If they win, it is understandable that candidates feel the victory reflects on their whole personality. Their relationship with the voters' verdict is direct. The managers, in contrast, are not being judged directly. They are involved in a less personal task; they are promoting the candidacy of someone else. They may, in fact, have promoted other candidates in the past. Their egos are probably not on the line. As a result, managers may be more willing to chalk up a victory or defeat to other factors—the candidate's ability to handle the media, the success of name recognition drives—more than to the candidate himself.

These ideas lend themselves to empirical testing. First, evidence will be presented to prove that candidates are more ego-involved than managers are. Several interview questions bear on involvement in the campaign. For example, respondents were asked: "Would you be satisfied if you (or, for managers: the candidate) won but just barely, or would you rather win big?" A candidate becomes an elected official, of course, whether he receives 50.1 percent of the vote or·85 percent, but many campaigners indicated that a big victory was necessary to satisfy their egos and make them feel secure with the voters and with their colleagues in office. The desire for a big victory can therefore be considered a sign of ego-involvement. While only 38 percent of the managers expressed a desire for a big victory, 50 percent of the candidates did so.

Further, campaigners were asked which they felt was more important to the campaign: media advertising or the candidate's personal appearances. It has already been shown that when managers are confident about the election results and about method-effectiveness, they are more likely to cut down on the candidate's personal campaigning than on the mass media. Managers are more likely than candidates to consider these personal appearances expendable. Table 3-2 presents candidates' and managers' responses. Objectively, of course, personal appearances by the candidate reach only a small proportion of the district, although his appearances do help generate newspaper and broadcast coverage of

Table 3-2
Are Media or Candidate's Appearances More Important?

	Candidates	Managers
Media are more important	19%	39%
Personal appearances are equally important or more important	81	61
	100%	100%
	N = 26	28

Note: Gamma is −.46.

his campaign. Yet four-fifths of the candidates consider their personal appearances at least as important as the far-reaching mass media. This is especially true of incumbents, although challengers show the tendency as well. Perhaps candidates attach a lot of importance to their personal appearances because they must justify the extensive amount of time and energy they put into the campaign. Or perhaps they believe the election is basically a judgment on their own abilities and character, and consequently that their personal contact must be as important to the voters as it is to the candidates themselves.

Similarly, when asked whether the voters in their district were more influenced by the candidate's image or by other factors such as party label or issues, most campaigners tended to emphasize the importance of the candidate. Only 11 percent of the managers considered other factors more important, as did 12 percent of the candidates. After the election was over, however, the candidates' views seemed to change a great deal. Their post-election responses to this question are presented in Table 3-3. After the election, still only 15 percent of managers said that factors other than the candidate's image were most important to the voters, but fully 48 percent of the candidates came to accept this view. The change in their attitudes seems to be due to the outcome of the election. When the responses of winning and losing candidates were compared, a majority (60 percent) of the winning candidates still considered image most important to the election result. A majority of losing candidates (53 percent)

Table 3-3
What Influenced Voters in the District: Post-Election View

	Candidates	Managers
Candidate's image	52%	85%
Other factors: party or issues	48	15
	100%	100%
	N = 25	26

Note: Gamma is −.67.

chose other factors instead. Many of the losing candidates, it seems, were reluctant to accept so much responsibility for the election outcome; instead they looked for something else to blame. Such a shift in attitude would protect the losing candidate's ego from the harsh questions raised by defeat. This response is consistent with the notion that candidates are more ego-involved in the campaign than managers.

Their ideas about fund-raising also reflect the candidates' greater personal involvement. Campaigners were asked whether people contribute to campaigns because they believe in certain issues or because they trust the candidate. Sixty-two percent of those who accepted the latter view were, in fact, the candidates. Most candidates disdained the idea that people contributed for reasons other than their belief in the candidate's personal abilities. A majority of those who felt contributors were expressing their views on issues were the managers. These findings all point to greater ego-involvement on the part of the candidates.

The candidates' greater personal involvement helps to explain why personality has more effect on candidates' decision-making than on managers'. But to complete the argument it is necessary to show that in general, ego-involvement allows personality traits to have more influence on behavior—or at least to be more consistent with attitudes and behavior.

To begin, it has often been demonstrated that related attitudes tend to be more consistent when an individual becomes personally involved with the subject of those attitudes. For example, Bernard Berelson and associates studied the feelings of voters in Elmira, New York, about the issues and personalities of the 1948 election.[13] They found that many voters who liked Harry Truman, but also favored the Taft-Hartley Act, perceived that Truman was in favor of the act. These people misperceived a well-publicized presidential stand. Perhaps they did so because the difference between their opinions on an important issue and those of their candidate caused them some psychological strain. Since they had become personally attached to Truman to the extent of favoring his candidacy, they solved the problem by deciding that his attitude toward Taft-Hartley was consistent with theirs. This tendency toward consistency in related attitudes has been noted by many social psychologists.[14] It causes beliefs that are valued weakly to be made consistent with beliefs held more strongly.

This strain toward consistency in a person's related attitudes increases when he has committed himself to an activity. For example, Jack W. Brehm and Arthur R. Cohen performed an experiment in which three groups of fraternity pledges worked at a boring job. One group had not been forced to participate in the task, another felt moderately coerced into doing it, and the third group felt they had definitely been forced to do the job. The first group had an inconsistent, not to mention unhappy, situation. They had volunteered but did not feel committed to the situation, the job was dull and they tended to dislike it. The situation of the third group was quite different. They expressed greater commitment to the task than the other groups did. And they tended to develop a positive attitude about it.[15] Since they had committed themselves personally, their attitudes came to be more consistent with their behavior. Similarly, two other studies found that being exposed to a campaign and learning more about it increase the consistency of one's political opinions.[16]

In short, the act of involvement has a forceful influence on an individual's attitudes. When participation and knowledge increase, attitudes and behavior relating to that involvement become more consistent. It seems reasonable that this will be especially true when the involvement is as personal as the candidate's decision to seek office. Even the most humble political candidate probably realizes that voters are judging him each time he acts. In a very real sense the process of being a candidate involves offering one's physical appearance, speaking ability, and leadership capacity to the voters for their approval or rejection, without ever knowing for certain the grounds on which the approval or rejection will be based. It would take a candidate of extraordinary inner strength to dissociate his own ego from these positive or negative judgments. In fact, the tendency of losing candidates to rationalize their defeat in terms of the inadequacy of the voters' information and intelligence, pointed out so well by John Kingdon, is quite understandable given the psychological strain candidates must face.[17]

The increase in split-ticket voting in the last decade further underlines the influence of the candidate's personality on the election results, and therefore increases the sense of responsibility a candidate must bear for his success or failure. It has been argued that voters are increasingly drifting away from their party loyalties, especially when voting for congressional or other higher offices. Certainly the importance of party identification has not evaporated. But as two observers contend, "today when people are asked how they make up their minds about a candidate, they discuss his general ability, his personality, his ability to handle the job, his stand on the issues, and so on."[18] It is harder for the candidate to escape personal involvement by laying victory or defeat at the door of the party. To summarize the argument, there is extensive support for the idea that there is a strain toward consistency in related attitudes, and that personal involvement increases that strain. Although this study cannot directly prove this point, it has been demonstrated in many other studies and there is reason to believe that it applies here. Data have been presented to show that candidates are more affectively involved in the campaign than managers are as a result of their spotlighted role. It would be expected that the candidates' personalities would have more influence on their attitudes and behavior than would be the case among managers. And this is actually true in one area of campaigning. The personality trait examined here—tolerance of ambiguity—was clearly more consistent with the related attitudes and behavior of the more involved campaigners: the candidates.

Tolerance and Information

We have seen the effects of this personality variable on the campaigners' willingness to accept change. It has been shown again that candidates and managers approach the campaign from different perspectives. But tolerance of ambiguity may also affect other important campaign decisions. For example, gathering information in a campaign can be a prelude to making changes in its operation. Even if the campaigner rejects changes and seeks information only to confirm his already-made decisions, he is still making himself vulnerable to surprises and bad news. We might expect that politicians who are more tolerant of ambiguity would be more likely to seek information than other politicians would.

A campaigner's information-seeking behavior was measured in several ways. Respondents were asked how they went about learning voters' opinions on the issues of the campaign. Two measures were derived from this question: first, whether or not they *did* seek such information, and second, how sophisticated and objective their information-gathering methods were. (Methods for seeking information were rated in four categories. Polls and canvassing were rated as the most sophisticated and objective; then, information coming from opinion leaders and the media; next, mailed questionnaires (which have typically low rates of response); and finally, intuition or no methods at all.) The campaigners were also asked specifically whether they used public opinion polls and canvassing.

To round out the measures, respondents were asked whether they invited the views of party leaders and newspaper political reporters about how the campaign was going. And campaigners were asked whether they sought information about their opponent's plans. The campaigners' level of tolerance was compared with the extent of their information-seeking in each of these seven categories. The results are shown in Table 3-4. Again a striking difference can be seen between

Table 3-4
Gamma Associations Between Tolerance and Information-Seeking

Methods of Seeking Information	Candidates	Managers
Asking voters about issues	−.35	.41
Sophistication of informational methods	−.63	.24
Public opinion polls	.27	−.06
Canvassing	−.23	.24
Asking party leaders about the campaign	−.02	.44
Asking newspapermen about the campaign	.37	.46
Information about opponent's plans	.25	.02

Note: Positive associations indicate that tolerant persons are more likely to seek information.

candidates and managers. Managers who are more tolerant of ambiguity are also generally open to new information. Only two of the relationships do not significantly support this finding among managers. One of these is the use of polls, which requires a sizable investment of money. Perhaps some tolerant managers were not able to use polling because of its cost. These positive relationships among managers still hold when incumbency, uncertainty, and party are held constant. But the associations between tolerance and information-seeking are stronger among challengers and those who are result-uncertain.

The picture is quite different among candidates. In three of the six significant relationships, the *less* tolerant candidates were more likely to seek information. These three items are important ones: the use of canvassing, whether voters' opinions are sought, and with what degree of sophistication or objectivity. Information is usually useful to a campaign organization. It is interesting that the same personality variable—tolerance of ambiguity—can lead to either a functional or a nonfunctional activity, depending on whether the personality belongs to a candidate or a manager.

This latest difference between the candidates and managers can be partly explained by looking at the ways they used information. The most obvious reason for gathering information is to resolve one's questions about some aspect of the campaign. There are certain types of questions that a campaigner needs to answer in order to do his job. He needs to know how good his chances are, how much more advertising may be needed in certain areas, where he can get more financial support, and many other important bits of knowledge. Gathering information in order to answer these questions can be considered an *instrumental* reason for seeking information. But a campaigner may also seek information for *expressive* purposes: to reassure himself that he is gaining support, to bolster the morale of his staff with positive reports, to give expression to his own feelings about the campaign or about his opponent, rather than to use the information to fill gaps in his knowledge.

The managers have been described as more pragmatic. Therefore they might be more concerned with the instrumental uses of information, while candidates might be more likely to seek information for expressive purposes. If this is true, a prediction based on these ideas can be tested.

If a person gathers information to answer questions about the campaign, this implies that he feels some uncertainty about the election result. It can be assumed that a campaigner who knows he will win or lose will not be as concerned with getting these answers. If managers are seeking information to fill holes in their knowledge about the campaign, then managers who feel result-uncertain ought to be more concerned with information-gathering than assured managers would. Similarly, if candidates are more likely to seek information for expressive purposes, their information-seeking should *not* be clearly related to uncertainty about the election. A result-assured candidate who is ego-involved in the campaign would have as much need to express himself and to confirm his beliefs as a result-uncertain candidate would. (Result-uncertainty might lead a candidate to seek more of the information that brings reassurance, however.)

It has already been shown (see Table 2-1) that the relationship between result-uncertainty and learning voters' views is very strong among managers. But there is only a weak association among candidates. While 75 percent of the uncertain managers sought voters' opinions on issues, only 31 percent of the assured managers did. The proportions of candidates who attempted to learn voters' views are 68 percent and 62 percent, respectively.

Relationships between result-uncertainty and other methods of information-seeking—polls, canvassing, the sophistication of methods used—show essentially the same results. These findings support the prediction about information-seeking. Uncertain managers respond pragmatically to their lack of information; they seek more. Uncertain candidates are not much more likely to gather information than assured candidates are. So information about public opinion and about the impact of the campaign seems to have different uses for candidates than for managers.

This conclusion is borne out by the campaigners' responses when asked about information-seeking. Most campaigners did give instrumental reasons for gathering information, but candidates gave about three times as many expressive reasons as managers did. Expressive reasons involved feelings about the campaign volunteers or party leaders, expressions of frustration with voters, the need to know that the opponent's campaign was foundering, and the need to see that people accepted the campaigner as a leader. Here are two examples of expressive responses by candidates:

Regarding the voters' feelings on issues:
Well, I guess maybe I'm not the kind of person who sits back trying to find out how they [the voters] feel and then tries to say the things that I think are going to please them. I think the responsibility of this job is more than that—and that's to make up my mind, and do it, and then explain why I've done it. In other words, to attempt to lead people along my thinking rather than reflect their currently-expressed ideas at a particular time.

Regarding the candidate's knowledge of his opponent's plans:
I think I'm a pretty good judge of this. Each two years I watch my opponent very closely. . . . But I still feel that people really—with six weeks to go in the campaign, people really don't know who he is, other than those he's met, has had a chance to talk to, may have left an impression on. But when you have 480,000 people in your district, you just cannot cover a district that way, except very superficially. Now if you're campaigning for the first time [as my opponent is], you may *think* you've met an awful lot of people. He hands out a little card saying, "You are the 41,273rd person that I've talked to in my campaign." Really, he's done this—which I disbelieve entirely. He probably started out with 40,000.

The first candidate is expressing his view that he has great capacity for leadership. The second, although he is assured that victory is likely, still looks for proof that his opponent is inept. It can be seen that many candidates seek information not just to trace the progress of the campaign but also to help them deal with their personal involvement in it.

These differences between candidates and managers help explain why their personalities relate differently to their information-seeking. Managers seem to gather information primarily to answer questions about the campaign. When they can tolerate ambiguous situations, they seek information from almost all available sources. When their personality is intolerant of ambiguity, they are not open to new information. Candidates have additional reasons for learning other people's views about the campaign. Some information, such as positive feedback from voters, can be used to restore their confidence or reassure their supporters. Perhaps candidates who are *intolerant* of ambiguity have a greater need for this kind of information because it is harder for them to adapt to the shifting, ambiguous cues of the campaign. It seems, then, that the original assumption about the relationship between personality and information-seeking must be modified. Tolerance of ambiguity apparently is positively associated with instrumental information-seeking, which is done by most campaigners. But tolerance is negatively related to expressive information-seeking. This is a hypothesis. It requires further study. But it provides a plausible explanation for the relationship between this personality trait and campaigners' interest in gathering new information.

To this point we have seen that tolerance of ambiguity affects campaigners' willingness to accept change and their willingness to gather information about the campaign. Now a further effect of personality will be explored: the style of the campaign.

Personality, Styles, and Goals

Describing the 1964 election, Karl A. Lamb and Paul A. Smith suggest that the personalities of the presidential candidates had an important impact on their styles of campaign decision-making. These authors found two kinds of styles in that election. An incremental style characterized the Johnson campaign, involving tolerance of inefficiency and confusion and a tendency to retain old workers and old methods, to use informal ways of gathering information, and to avoid a rigidly organized schedule. The Goldwater campaign, on the other hand, was a rationalized, formal operation. It tended toward intolerance of ambiguity, a determination to search for the most up-to-date methods of learning voter preferences and to comprehensively evaluate all possible plans for greatest efficiency. Lamb and Smith call it a comprehensive style.[19]

These two styles in many ways represent the traditional struggle of any campaign: the ideal of efficiency pulling against the daily buildup of disorganization. Lamb and Smith point out that the campaigner's style is not determined minute by minute, but is heavily directed by his experience and personality. They report the statement of one of Goldwater's closest advisers that "a physicist who knows the laws of gravity is not going to step off a roof. Goldwater believed in certain things. This made his decisions easy. There was never anything hard for Goldwater in making decisions."[20] Other campaigners, evidently not physicists, do of course step off the roof with astonishing regularity. So personality and background help to guide the decisions of campaigners toward greater organization or more informal activity.

Again this provides an opportunity to test whether personality traits have as much influence on managers' decisions as they do on candidates'. The Wisconsin campaigners can be examined to learn whether different styles of campaigning exist, and whether the choice of style is related to personality. Eight measures have been chosen to represent the major characteristics of the incremental and comprehensive styles.

The comprehensive style involves a willingness to search for new methods and personnel, while incrementalists tend to rely on tradition. These qualities can be tested by questions on the use of the same methods as in previous campaigns, and the degree of worker turnover. The comprehensive style is further described as using the most up-to-date means of learning public opinion. Questions on the use of public opinion polls and the sophistication of methods for tapping voters' views represent this dimension. Another question, labelled "flexibility," asks whether respondents feel a campaigner should stick to his original plan or whether he should respond to events as they occur. The latter choice would reflect the incremental style. Two other items ask whether the campaign organization is run formally or informally, and whether the budget is allocated according to rules of efficiency or not. The latter question asks if the campaign is budgeting any items that, in the respondent's view, could be cut without losing votes (labelled "cut anything").

If these two styles exist, a matrix should show strong positive relationships among these measures. If the choice of style is related to personality, strong relationships should be found with the respondents' tolerance of ambiguity. A matrix of these measures is presented in Table 3-5.

Two conclusions can be drawn from this matrix. First, these eight measures do not interrelate strongly. The two styles of campaigning cannot be seen clearly in the attitudes and behavior of either the candidates or the managers. There are indications that the styles do exist in part—most of the relationships are positive and some are even quite strong—but the evidence is weak that some campaigners are down-the-line incrementalists while others are diehard comprehensivists.[a]

We can also see clearly in Table 3-5 that the candidates' tolerance of

[a]Another matrix shows, however, that campaigners do separate into those using primarily New Politics methods and those who rely on more traditional methods. The interrelationships are especially strong among managers.

Table 3-5
Gamma Matrix of Incremental and Comprehensive Styles

Candidates	2	3	4	5	6	7	8
1. Tolerance	−.34	.30	−.27	.63	.63	.62	.22
2. Same methods	−						
3. Worker turnover	.14	−					
4. Polls	.57	.16	−				
5. Good methods	−.22	.38	.23	−			
6. Flexibility	.08	.00	.18	.56	−		
7. Informal organization	−.78	.08	−.06	.51	.21	−	
8. Cut anything	−.16	.00	−.39	.32	.43	.19	−
Managers							
1. Tolerance	−.11	−.71	.06	−.24	.26	−.46	−.01
2. Same methods	−						
3. Worker turnover	.85	−					
4. Polls	.17	.58	−				
5. Good methods	.01	.35	.38	−			
6. Flexibility	.22	−.19	.23	−.22	−		
7. Informal organization	−.25	−.18	.43	.01	.36	−	
8. Cut anything	−.32	−.18	−.60	.14	.31	−.14	−

Note: These eight variables stem from the following interview questions that can be found in the appendix: variable (1) the personality test; (2) question 5; (3) question 9a; (4) question 6a; (5) rating of the sophistication of methods named in response to question 17a; (6) question 15; (7) question 9c; (8) question 23a.

ambiguity strongly influences their choice of campaign style. Managers do not show this pattern. While Lamb and Smith suggest that a tolerant personality is likely to choose the incremental style (and this is true of candidates), the tolerant *managers* are more likely to choose elements of the comprehensive style. Yet the comprehensive style implies that the respondent wants to rationalize his campaign in order to avoid ambiguity and inefficiency. In other words, there is no consistency between personality and decision-making style among managers. The size of the relationships is smaller and less consistent than those found among candidates. Again, we find that managers often behave and perceive campaigning quite differently than their personalities would suggest. This provides further evidence that the personalities of candidates are more involved in their decision-making than managers' personalities are.

Tolerance of ambiguity has more impact on campaigners' theories about campaigning than it does on the content of their actual decisions. For example, tolerance is not related to the number of methods used in the campaign, nor to the types of campaign techniques chosen. Intolerant campaigners are no less likely than tolerants to use Old Politics methods such as personal appearances, even though such methods are less easily controlled and organized than are television and radio or newspaper advertisements.

Tolerant and intolerant campaigners do differ, however, in their theories about running a campaign. Respondents were asked whether the campaign should concentrate on the independent voters or on the candidate's likely supporters. We might expect that persons intolerant of ambiguity would prefer to target their efforts toward their supporters, since the decisions of the independent voters would be much harder to predict. In fact this is the case, particularly among candidates, who seem to have a stronger need for reassurance about their support.

Regarding the major function of the campaign, tolerance of ambiguity also makes a difference. Campaigners were asked to choose whether educating the voters or electing a man to office is the main goal of the campaign. Again candidates and managers were affected differently. It would seem that people with a limited tolerance for ambiguity would believe that their primary function is to elect a man to office. As many politicians have pointed out, the alternative goal of educating the voters is frustrating, difficult, and often likely to produce indeterminate or negative results. The managers did respond as predicted. All of the intolerant managers opted for electing a man to office. Among candidates, on the other hand, the only significant support for educating the voters came from the intolerant respondents. While a plurality (43 percent) of the intolerant candidates opted for electing the candidate, fully 29 percent felt that educating the voters is more important, and another 29 percent judged both functions equally important. (Gammas for this relationship are .46 for candidates and .54 for managers.)

What accounts for this candidate-manager difference on the all-important question of the purpose of campaigning? In several tests of tolerance of ambiguity, it was found that the intolerant candidates tended to be more ego-involved than were their more tolerant colleagues. Perhaps intolerant candidates do not like the idea that voters make ambiguous judgments based on "images" and prefer that they be led to vote on the basis of a clearly-defined issue position. Perhaps intolerant candidates prefer the leader-follower relationship to go in one direction only: as one candidate stated above, for the leader to instruct his followers without having to bend to their ideas. Or perhaps intolerant candidates try to protect their feelings against the damage of possible defeat by redefining their goal. In this last case, a defeated candidate could then console himself with the belief that he did at least try to educate the voters. This consolation would have been useful, since intolerant candidates were significantly more likely to lose the 1970 election than the tolerant candidates were. In short, the candidates' greater ego-involvement probably affects this relationship between personality and attitudes about election goals.

The managers, on the other hand, gave less complex and more goal-directed answers. Intolerant managers may feel the need of a clearly defined win-or-lose goal, while more of the tolerant managers are able to concentrate on the task of educating voters on issues.

Attitudes toward fund-raising are also affected by personality. The more tolerant the campaigner, the more likely he is to state that contributors give because they believe in certain issues rather than because they trust the candidate. Tolerance seems to help a campaigner accept the idea that contributors may be working for some larger cause, rather than just his own personal success. Again, the strength of the relationships shows that the personality trait has more impact on candidates' beliefs than on managers'. The fact that a contributor could be motivated by something other than trust in the candidate is evidently a much harder blow to the intolerant candidates than to the intolerant managers. (Gammas for this relationship are .42 for candidates and .24 for managers.)

It is worth noting that managers' scores on the personality test show them to be somewhat more tolerant of ambiguity than candidates are. Table 3-6 shows the distribution of scores. If candidates are less able to accept ambiguity, and if ambiguity is ever-present in campaigns, it seems that managers are better able to adapt to this aspect of the campaign situation than candidates are. Further information about the problems of adaptation and the different strains faced by candidates and managers will be discussed in Chapter 4.

This difference in tolerance between candidates and managers does not result from different amounts of political experience. Tolerance of ambiguity is not related to experience—either in public office or in managing a campaign. It bears no relationship to the type of office the campaigner is seeking—statewide or congressional. Because there is no real difference in experience between tolerant and intolerant campaigners, tolerance does not seem to be a condition for political success (even though it may facilitate *participation*). Intolerant campaigners seem as able to survive in politics as tolerant persons are. Tolerant campaigners were more likely to win the 1970 election, however. This might mean that a trend is developing toward the election of tolerant people, or that tolerant campaigners stay in office a shorter time and therefore have no more experience in politics than intolerant persons do.

Table 3-6
Personality Test Scores of Candidates and Managers

Test Score (Trichotomized)	Candidates	Managers
Most tolerant of ambiguity	37%	45%
Somewhat tolerant	37	41
Least tolerant	26	14
	100%	100%
N =	27	29

Note: Gamma is .21.

There is an especially interesting relationship between personality and party. Democrats tend to be more tolerant of ambiguity than Republicans are. (Gammas for this relationship are .19 for candidates and .48 for managers.) Thus, representatives of the two parties differ clearly on a philosophical question that relates to liberal-conservative differences: the acceptance of change. The liberal-conservative dimension has often been thought to separate leaders of the two parties, even though it does not appear strongly in the political opinions of the general public. For example, the research of Herbert McClosky suggests that Democratic leaders are much more accepting of change than Republican leaders are.[21]

Therefore these data support the proposition that party differences have a clear ideological base among party activists. But further, the responses of the Wisconsin campaigners indicate that this ideological difference may be rooted to some extent in personality differences. A party difference that is related to personality may prove to be more enduring than if the division were based solely on issues. Perhaps these ideological divisions are found more often among party leaders than among other citizens because the party leaders are more politically involved, and consequently their beliefs are more consistent with their related personality traits. These findings bring up another interesting question. Ambiguity is common in American campaigns, and Democrats are more tolerant of ambiguity. Are the Democrats better adapted to the nature of American campaigning, and therefore more likely to remain the majority party in the long run?

Summary and Conclusions

This chapter presents strong evidence that one personality trait—tolerance of ambiguity—affects the attitudes and behavior of campaigners. Its effects are especially strong among candidates. For instance, there is a stable, orderly relationship between candidates' level of tolerance and their willingness to accept change. Similarly, although the incremental and comprehensive styles were not clearly found here, the candidates' personalities did relate strongly and consistently with most elements of these styles. In general, managers' tolerance of ambiguity does not relate as consistently or as strongly to their campaign decision-making.

It has been proposed that candidates' personalities are more influential in their decision-making because candidates tend to be more personally involved in the campaign than managers are. This personal or ego-involvement increases the likelihood that personality will serve as a screen for beliefs and choices made in the campaign. Managers' tolerance of ambiguity is much less consistent with their attitudes and activities, it is suggested, because their involvement is more pragmatic and less personal.

The relationship between tolerance and information-seeking is more complex.

Tolerance tends to promote information-seeking among managers more than among candidates. This difference between candidates and managers may relate to differences in the ways they use information. Managers seek information when the knowledge they need to have about the election is incomplete. Candidates, in addition to trying to fill gaps in their understanding, also seek information for expressive purposes. Information can provide candidates with support for their beliefs about voters, opponents, and the proper ways to conduct a campaign. It can provide reassurance. Candidates more than managers use information to help them manage their emotional involvement in the election.

Tolerance of ambiguity also affects the theories that campaigners hold about elections. Tolerant persons are more likely to accept the idea that a campaign must concentrate on independents rather than the candidate's supporters. Tolerants are also better able to state that contributors are motivated by a belief in certain issues rather than by the appeal of the candidate's personality. The evidence indicates that intolerant campaigners are more likely to require strong personal dedication from the voters, while tolerant persons tend to accept any degree of support, in any form.

These results raise questions about the meaning of a campaigner's involvement in an election. Is personal involvement a good thing or a bad thing for democracy? If many candidates are strongly ego-involved, are they able to dissociate themselves from the campaign enough so that if they lose, they can accept the loss without outrage? Chong Lim Kim, in a study of state legislative candidates, finds that election losers do retain support for the system, but that their support diminishes.[22] It would be useful to learn whether the support of the more emotionally involved candidates decreases more, if they lose, than that of the less involved candidates. If so, it would be important to identify the conditions under which their support for democratic rules of the game could reach a dangerously low level.

Although tolerance of ambiguity does not affect the number or type of campaign techniques used and is not related to political experience or incumbency, it is found more frequently among Democrats and managers. This difference among party leaders lends support, and a possible explanation, to studies reporting that party differences among political leaders are related to ideological differences.

The greater ability of managers to tolerate ambiguity recalls a serious problem. If candidates' decisions in elections are guided by personality factors, then the candidates' ability to respond to changes in public opinion may be hampered. More evidence on the influence of campaigners' attitudes and perceptions on their decision-making will be examined in Chapter 4.

4

Organization and Disorganization

Campaigns are socio-political systems writ small.[1] Campaigns have power relationships just as a political system does. Campaigns have internal conflicts, negotiations, and decision-making processes, although they do not have the capacity to enforce their decisions (even on other staff members) that a polity has. And like other social systems, campaigns have goals, patterns of interaction and communication, assigned tasks, and identifiable boundaries.

Individual campaign organizations, in short, exhibit a great deal of complexity. We have seen that different types of uncertainty and differences in personality traits contribute to the variety of responses found among campaigns. As an organization becomes more complex and more differentiated, it is likely to need general rules, norms, or traditions to guide its members and help them handle the problems posed by their work. To provide a clearer picture of the campaign as a functioning social and political organization, this chapter will focus on the forces that help organize campaigns—the general norms and rules of campaigning (as opposed to specific norms that apply only to particular subgroups of campaigners), and the forces that threaten organization—the stresses and pressures on the participants.

If there is a set of rules or norms that applies to all campaigners, then the job of understanding their campaigns would become much easier. By simply discovering these rules, an observer could predict the basic outlines of any given campaign, at least in general terms. Alternatively, if there are few such general norms, it might be possible to study campaign structure from a different perspective; there might be sets of special norms that guide the behavior of particular kinds of campaigners, such as incumbents or Democrats or managers.

At a very general level, campaigns do seem to obey certain rules. For example, the ways in which a candidate can appeal to the voters are limited. He can be expected to consider using television, radio, newspapers and brochures if he has the money. But most people would be surprised to see him advertising his good points in church, or on the pages of *Playboy*. American society puts certain constraints on the politician so that political activity is considered appropriate in some settings and inappropriate in others. But these and other constraints, including the size of the district, the party identification of voters, and the amount of money available, are general enough to permit many different kinds of campaigns to be developed.

Take, for instance, the candidate's relationship with his staff. This is an important aspect of campaigning, and one might expect to find traditions and general rules dictating that certain patterns be followed. But the 1972 Nixon and McGovern campaigns provided two very different patterns of candidate-staff interaction, as many recent presidential contests have.[2] Although the two national campaigns faced the same constituency and worked within the same setting, their styles of organization were radically different. The Committee to Re-Elect the President (CRP) organized into a businesslike hierarchy and developed structures that insulated the candidate from the campaign. It was more effective, the staff felt, for Richard Nixon to be seen as a working president, not a presidential candidate. A score of cabinet members and Republican leaders were designated "presidential surrogates" by the campaign organization. Their function was to represent the president and to assume the burden of most speaking invitations that would normally come to the White House. Because so many spokesmen for the president were available, they could also be used to mount a broad, coordinated attack on the proposals of the opposition. The hierarchy in CRP and the surrogate system shielded the candidate from demands by persons active in the campaign, as well as from voters. Away from the pressure of the campaign, the candidate did not become involved in staff problems or conflicts. This pattern of isolation seems to have characterized Richard Nixon's prior four years as president.[3]

In contrast, the McGovern campaign did not generate a strong organization in the general election. Plagued by indecision, beginning with the question of replacing vice-presidential candidate Thomas Eagleton, the campaign produced an image of whirling confusion. In particular, there was a struggle between party leaders and McGovern loyalists regarding the direction of the campaign. The candidate was in contact with many key staff members on a daily basis, and at times even helped to mediate the disagreements among them. Many activist organizations were able to transmit their demands through sympathetic staff members to the candidate himself. Members of a gay activist group making an effort to garner the candidate's support, for example, were admitted to several press conferences by a friendly McGovern staffer, even though association with gay activism is not generally regarded as very helpful to any politician.

Though competing for the same office, one candidate was insulated by a hierarchy of staff members and the other was besieged not only by the voters but by members of his staff as well.[4] Let us, however, turn to the Wisconsin campaigns. Do they have many general rules in common, or are there variations as great as those in the 1972 presidential campaigns?

Patterns of Beliefs about Campaign Organization

Candidates and managers express long lists of preferences about the way a campaign should be conducted. If these preferences tend to be widely agreed upon, then they could be called general norms of campaigning. Norms, to paraphrase Talcott Parsons, are general patterns of expectations that define the specific expectations of persons in a given organization.[5] For example, if an organization (such as Congress) requires new members to maintain a low profile initially while learning the rules from older members, then observers and members alike could anticipate that any newcomer would be expected to follow that path. If the new member broke the rule, the organization would be expected to apply certain punishments, or negative sanctions (for example, social isolation or reprimands from members) that would encourage him to reconsider and accept the norm.

In short, norms communicate the general values of a group of people in an operational way. Group members can then develop sets of expectations about the activities and the values of different persons or roles with whom they will be in contact. Norms make the work of an organization more predictable, both to the observer and the insider.

Writers have disagreed about whether there are norms of campaigning. Some suggest that these norms do exist,[6] while others feel that beliefs about campaigning are not specific enough, and are not followed regularly enough to be called norms.[7] For example, Ira Sharkansky states that political decision rules are too vague to guide behavior. A decision rule focuses attention on a limited number of considerations in order to simplify decision-making. But this is not likely in politics, says Sharkansky, for many reasons. Politics cannot be standardized. Voter response to different campaign techniques cannot be predicted. Candidates vary in background, skills and standards. Strategies must therefore be personalized. Decision rules will not become generally accepted.[8]

Similarly, in a summary of beliefs about campaigns, Austin Ranney and Willmoore Kendall illustrate the point that politicians agree only on very general rules. For example: (1) the candidate should always stay on the offensive and should avoid responding to attacks on his record or personal integrity; (2) voters gravitate toward candidates with attractive personalities and shun candidates with unattractive personalities; and (3) voters vote *against* rather than *for*, so a candidate should try not to antagonize any potential supporters.[9] These rules sound like sage advice for a would-be officeholder, but they are not specific enough to serve as guides for his behavior. How does a candidate avoid antagonizing potential supporters? What constitutes "staying on the offensive," and how aggressive must a candidate be to fulfill this prescription? When it comes down to cases, agreement on these broad prescriptions often dwindles.

To determine whether certain beliefs can be considered norms, the Wisconsin campaigners' attitudes and theories about the conduct of a campaign will be examined. Two tests will be applied to these attitudes and theories. First, a particular attitude must be widely accepted by campaigners. Second, the attitude must have a clear relationship with the campaigners' behavior in that area. Beliefs and attitudes, of course, are abstractions and cannot be seen directly. But by looking at the campaigners' reported behavior, we can see whether norms are operating.[10]

The Wisconsin respondents were asked many questions about the best methods of conducting a campaign. Beginning with the goal of the campaign, they were asked, "In general terms, now, do you think a campaign should primarily educate people about the issues, or should it primarily elect a man to office?" Their responses are presented in Table 4-1. The table shows general agreement that the campaign's goal is to elect the candidate, not to educate the voters. Candidates agreed with managers on this question. So at least one belief is accepted widely enough to be called a norm. But there is less agreement on how this goal—electing the candidate—is to be achieved.

Respondents were asked whether the campaign should concentrate its efforts on uncommitted voters or those who are likely to support the candidate, or both. The results are shown in Table 4-2. Most managers said that the campaign should concentrate on the independents. For many candidates, however, the question could only be answered by "both." The three options attracted nearly equal numbers of candidates.

When asked (during the campaign) whether voters choose a candidate on the basis of the candidate's image or his party label, a belief relevant to the choice of campaign emphasis, responses were given as presented in Table 4-3. It is interesting that most of these campaigners do not accept a belief that has been

Table 4-1
Beliefs about the Goal of the Campaign

Campaigns Should Primarily	Candidates	Managers
Educate the voters on issues	14%	10%
Elect a man to office	71	79
Do both (refused to choose)	14	10
	99%	99%
	N = 28	29

Table 4-2
Beliefs about the Proper Target for the Campaign

Campaign's Target Should Be	Candidates	Managers
Independents, uncommitted voters	41%	66%
Likely supporters	26	24
Both	33	10
	100%	100%
	N = 27	29

Table 4-3
Beliefs about Determinants of Voters' Choice in Elections

Choice Is Based On	Candidates	Managers
Candidate's image	62%	79%
Candidate's party label	12	11
Both, don't know	27	11
	101%	101%
	N = 26	28

generally assumed by political scientists: that politicians feel most votes are determined by party identification.[11] Managers largely agreed that the candidate's image is most important to the voters, but the candidates were not as certain.

In these three tables, the managers reached a higher level of consensus than the candidates did. Managers also had less difficulty making a choice on the questions than candidates did. About one-third of the candidates could not (or did not feel they should) make a choice between the responses to each question, as opposed to only about one in ten managers. On these three vital campaign questions, in summary, the managers' beliefs are sufficiently uniform to be called norms: that the campaigner must be out to win, must concentrate on the independents, and must emphasize the candidate's image. Among candidates, agreement is not as widespread and there is some reluctance to narrow the campaign's objectives by making these choices.

Turning to beliefs about campaign communication, the respondents were asked to rate party leaders and newspapermen as sources of information about the campaign. The results for this item are presented in Table 4-4. Although party leaders and newspaper reporters are often in contact with campaigns, a majority of campaigners did not consider party leaders and newspapermen to be trustworthy sources of information. However, their attitudes about information sources cannot be called general norms, because large minorities dissent in each case.

Finally, the campaigners were asked about the amount of flexibility a candidate ought to have. Table 4-5 presents their responses. This table shows that candidates approve of flexibility less than the managers do. This finding supports similar results reported in the last chapter. But the level of agreement on flexibility in campaigning is not high enough to reveal a campaign norm.

Candidates and managers did agree strongly on one further question. Respondents were asked whether any kinds of activities or appeals to voters were improper in a campaign. The answers tended to center around two main types of campaign practices. Mudslinging, name-calling, and similar activities were considered improper by 73 percent of candidates and 75 percent of

Table 4-4
Beliefs about the Value of Two Sources of Information

Party Leaders Are	Candidates	Managers
Good source	33%	22%
Depends, don't know	7	18
Not good source	59	59
	99%	99%
	N = 27	27
Newspapermen Are		
Good source	33%	25%
Depends, don't know	4	14
Not good source	62	61
	99%	100%
	N = 24	28

Table 4-5
Beliefs about the Value of Flexibility

Candidate Should	Candidates	Managers
Be flexible	43%	43%
Be partly flexible, partly stick to plan	29	39
Stick to original plan	29	18
	101%	100%
	N = 28	28

managers. In addition, 24 percent of candidates and 32 percent of managers stated that playing on people's fears about racial or religious differences was improper. (Multiple answers were permitted, so percentages total more than 100 percent for this question.)

To this point, only two beliefs were accepted by enough of *both* candidates and managers to be called norms of campaigning. About three-quarters of the respondents agreed that winning the election is the primary goal of the campaign and that mudslinging is not a proper campaign activity (although, as one candidate candidly pointed out, "We don't believe in mudslinging. Or let's say this: if you've got mud to throw, the candidate can't be the one who does it. Someone else in the campaign. . . .").

Managers, however, did reach a high level of agreement on other questions as well. This seems to indicate that there are additional norms in campaigns but they apply only to managers. Evidence on this subject will be discussed in the next chapter. But first, let us look at the relationships between beliefs and behavior, to determine whether any norms can actually be seen in operation.

Do These Beliefs Govern
Campaigners' Behavior?

If norms are mutual expectations about people's values and actions, it seems reasonable to assume that these norms will be reflected in the behavior of group members. If the norms actually guide behavior, they would provide greater structure to the campaign. In order to determine whether such structure exists, campaigners were asked about their activities in areas related to their theories of campaigning.[a] In cases where valid reports of behavior were difficult or impossible to obtain, beliefs were compared with other beliefs on the same subject, on the assumption that an attitude that is expressed consistently is more likely to guide behavior.

Beginning with the most widely accepted beliefs, respondents' views about the goal of the campaign were found to be strongly associated with a related attitude—whether educating the voters is desirable or feasible in campaigns. Among both candidates and managers the association was perfect: 1.00.[b] No data were available on the amount of mudslinging done by the campaigners, however, since the campaigns were not monitored continuously and the definition of mudslinging generally depends on who is throwing the mud. So the actual strength of the prohibition against mudslinging cannot be measured.

Some consistency was also found regarding communication patterns. Campaigners who considered party leaders or newspapermen a good source of information were much more likely to actually consult these sources during the campaign than were campaigners who did not consider them good sources. Finally, campaigners believing that a candidate should remain flexible during the campaign were significantly more likely to run informal campaigns, leaving room for flexibility rather than organizing their staff around a comprehensive plan. Then, three kinds of beliefs do give structure to behavior. Beliefs about the goal of the campaign, the value of different information sources, and the need for flexibility all relate to campaigners' attitudes or behavior in the same areas.

Beyond these three areas of congruence, however, the association between beliefs and behavior, or beliefs and related beliefs, declines markedly. For example, it is widely assumed that television is the medium that best reaches the uncommitted voter.[12] We might expect that campaigners who want to concentrate on uncommitted voters would use more television than would campaigners who prefer to aim at their likely supporters. Among the Wisconsin candidates this was not the case. Candidates who believed in concentrating on the

---

[a]Note that these are campaigners' *reports* of behavior rather than observations of their actual behavior. These self-reports may be slanted in certain ways. For example, a respondent may report his behavior as more, rather than less, congruent with his expressed beliefs.

[b]Gamma reaches its maximum (± 1.00) when one cell in a 2 x 2 table, or two cells in a 3 x 2 table are empty. The latter is the case here, so that while all candidates and managers who see education as the campaign's main function feel education is desirable, 33 percent of candidates and 53 percent of managers believing that *electing the candidate* is the campaign's main goal *also* feel that education is desirable.

uncommitted used *less* television than did candidates who were more concerned with their own supporters, and much less television than candidates who aimed for both groups. Among managers there was no relationship between these two beliefs. Similarly, those who felt that one should target the campaign at supporters did not use more bumperstickers, signs, or other material generally associated with reinforcing one's own side.[13] In fact, the opposite occurred. Campaigners who believed in concentrating on the uncommitted used much more of this collateral material. And although many writers have suggested that the uncommitted voters are more attuned to image campaigns, there was no significant relationship between targeting the campaign at uncommitted voters and stating that the candidate's image is most important to voters.[14]

In summary, some of the beliefs tested are clearly consistent with behavior or related attitudes, but many are not. Only two beliefs met the original criterion that they be widely accepted by both candidates and managers; only one of these fulfilled the second criterion that the belief be consistent with behavior or related beliefs. The other could not be tested against actual behavior. Other beliefs about campaigning were not held widely enough or consistently enough to be called norms. So only two of the general beliefs studied (at most) actually structured the attitudes and behavior of most campaigners. Why is there such a weak (or negative) relationship between other beliefs and actual campaigning?

There are three main reasons why campaigns are structured by only a small number of general norms. First, it has been stated that norms have negative sanctions or perceived punishments that result when a norm is disobeyed. In the case of a social club, a boisterous member might be sanctioned by being shut out of conversations, or by direct admonitions from other members. In a campaign there is one sanction that stands out from all the others. The clearest negative sanction, the strongest punishment, is losing the election. This sanction can only be applied by the voters. But contrary to most social clubs, there are no real guidelines telling the politician how to avoid that sanction. Voters may turn thumbs down on a campaign for many different kinds of reasons, many of which the campaigner will probably never learn about.

Campaigners did not seem to associate many specific kinds of campaign behavior with negative sanctions. The interview questions usually brought prompt and often lengthy responses. But when respondents were asked what campaign activities or appeals were improper, most were very slow to answer. In part this may reflect the campaigners' reluctance to talk in negative terms, but it also points out that very few campaign behaviors are clearly linked in the campaigners' minds with negative sanctions.

The two campaign norms accepted by both candidates and managers *did* seem clearly related in their minds to the sanction of losing the election. Many campaigners suggested that only losers would run an "educational campaign." And those who considered mudslinging improper often noted that it could backfire on the candidate using it, causing voters to sympathize with the candidate under attack. References to mudslinging were often accompanied by phrases such as "and I'd never do it myself," indicating that a charge of mudslinging could be harmful to a victory-minded politician. But there was no consensus, for example, that choosing to concentrate on uncommitted voters as opposed to one's supporters would lead to defeat or victory. Many choices were not clearly associated with winning or losing. Consequently norms are not likely to develop in many areas of campaigning for there are no sanctions to ensure that campaigners will follow the norms.

A second factor that works against the development of strong norms is the influence of personality on the campaigners' attitudes and behavior. It has been demonstrated, for example, that a campaigner's tolerance of ambiguity affects his willingness to make changes in the campaign. If flexibility is related to the personality trait of tolerance of ambiguity, then a norm encouraging flexibility cannot be expected to have much influence on campaigners who are *not* tolerant of ambiguity. If politics tended to attract people willing to accept widely-held campaign beliefs regardless of their own personal preferences, this would not be the case. But especially among candidates, we have found that personality *does* affect attitudes and behavior.

Third, strong norms are unlikely because campaigners bring different experiences to the election, and these experiences affect their judgment about the way a campaign should be run. John H. Kessel provides an example when he discusses Barry Goldwater's 1964 decision to have a highly organized presidential campaign staff. In 1960, when Goldwater was chairman of the Senate Republican Campaign Committee, the organization of presidential candidate Richard Nixon was housed in several different buildings. In his discussion, Kessel quotes Goldwater: " 'I wanted to contact Bob Finch [Nixon's 1960 campaign director, now lieutenant governor of California] ,' Sen. Goldwater once recalled. 'I called five different headquarters. There wasn't one where the telephone operator knew who Bob Finch was!' To the Senator's mind, this was a symptom of the problems of a split organization. He wanted to have a unified campaign organization," to avoid what he considered to be Nixon's mistake.[15]

Just as previous campaign experiences make a difference, campaigners' occupational experiences can also influence their beliefs about elections. For example, the respondents' occupations were found to affect their feelings about different sources of information. Although the numbers here are small, all the full-time party workers (there were eight) considered party leaders a good source for campaign information and also consulted with party leaders. Similarly, there was a perfect association between trusting newspapermen and actually using them as information sources among the two campaigner-journalists who responded to these questions. In fact, when one manager was asked what source he would trust most, he replied:

Now I don't know why, but firemen are a good source. They seem to get around. I don't know what it is about firemen and policemen, but they do get around . . . maybe it's because of their jobs. When they talk about the economy, they're concerned with salaries, with where the money's coming from, having so much welfare . . .

The speaker is, not surprisingly, a firefighter. After long periods of contact with other people in a profession, it is understandable that their feelings and common experiences would influence a campaigner's beliefs.

The experience of winning or losing also affects respondents' feelings about running a campaign. Looking at their beliefs about the factors that determine people's votes, Table 4-6 compares campaigners' pre-election opinions with their post-election answers to the same question. Many candidates and managers changed their minds about this question. Many who had considered image most important before the election switched to other factors after the election was over. Those who chose party during the campaign changed their minds and said, after election day, that image was most important to the voters. Candidates were especially likely to change their opinions. Half of the candidates who chose image during the campaign changed their views after the election was over, compared with only one in five managers.[c]

According to the persuasive argument of John Kingdon, the election result *causes* these changes. Losing candidates, he contends, feel the need to rationalize their defeat. They do so by accepting the view that voters follow party labels like so many sheep. On the other hand, the winners tend to congratulate themselves by stating that voters are guided by the candidate's personal qualities,

Table 4-6
Determinants of Voters' Choice: Pre- and Post-Election Views

Attitude after Election Day	Attitude During Campaign					
	Candidates			Managers		
	Image	Both	Party	Image	Both	Party
Image was most important	50%	50%	100%	81%	100%	100%
Other factors were more important (including party and issues)	50	50	0	19	0	0
	100%	100%	100%	100%	100%	100%
	N = 14	6	3	21	2	2

Note: Gamma is −.42 for candidates and −1.00 for managers.

[c]During the campaign the respondents were given only two options on this question: image or party. In the post-election questionnaire, because the interviews indicated that many respondents considered the issues of the campaign important to voters, this option was added. Although the change does add information, it limits the comparability of the pre- and post-election responses.

not by a party habit.[16] Table 4-7 tests this argument by comparing the respondents' post-election beliefs about the voters' choices with the actual election results. These results are an interesting variation on Kingdon's. Section A of this table shows that winning candidates were somewhat more likely to choose image, but there is no relationship among managers. Looking at the other determinants of votes, however, Section B shows that the winning campaigners were more likely to say that the *issues* of the campaign were most important to voters, while the losers tended to choose party identification. If we follow Kingdon's argument, then the issues were even more important to these campaigners than were the voters' feelings about the candidates' personal qualities. The winners were able to preserve their modesty by attributing their victory to the issues they raised rather than to their personalities. And the losers believed that voters blindly followed party labels rather than rejecting the issue positions of the losing campaigners. The difference between these results and Kingdon's might be due to the fact that Kingdon's interviews were conducted five to six months after election day, while these post-election questionnaires were administered right after the election. The full impact of winning or losing may not set in until some time has passed. The campaigners' rationalizations may build over several months.

To conclude, only two of the beliefs studied are widely accepted by the

Table 4-7
Determinants of Voters' Choice and Winning or Losing

Section A: Candidate's Image	Candidates		Managers	
	Won	Lost	Won	Lost
Image was most important	60%	47%	83%	86%
Other factors were more important	40	53	17	14
	100%	100%	100%	100%
	N = 10	15	12	14
	gamma = .26		−.09	
Section B: Other factors				
Issues of the campaign	62%	25%	75%	43%
Party identification	25	58	12	43
Other	12	17	12	14
	99%	100%	99%	100%
	N = 8	12	8	7
	gamma = .51		.47	

Note: Several respondents chose two or more factors as most important when answering the post-election questionnaire. Therefore, Section A classifies respondents according to whether image was one of their choices or not, and Section B looks at choices other than image.

campaigners and are clearly consistent with related attitudes or behavior, and therefore can be called general norms of campaigning. These beliefs are very basic. They deal with the goal of the campaign and the avoidance of an improper activity. There may be other general campaign norms that this study did not test. The finding that there are few *general* norms does *not* imply that individual campaigns do not have their own sets of rules, expectations, and structures. Many do—several campaigners (largely incumbents) said that they preferred an elaborate organization. In addition this finding does not imply that there are no *specialized* norms that apply to subgroups of campaigners. We have already seen that incumbents behave differently from challengers, and candidates behave differently from managers. This chapter points out that managers reach agreement on particular beliefs to a greater extent than candidates do, and consequently that more norms appear to apply to the managers.

It *has* been demonstrated, however, that campaigning is not an institution such as Congress where a newcomer enters a highly structured social system. A new campaigner does not appear to learn a set of norms that all other campaigners will also follow, beyond the very basics of running for office. Therefore it is hard for him to form expectations about other campaigners, including his opponent, except on the basis of what they have done in the past. This scarcity of general norms is due to three factors: differences in the campaigners' previous experiences, the strong influence of personality on campaigning, and the lack of sure knowledge about the way to win an election.

Stress on the Campaign Organization

Even if campaigns do not share many general norms, they do have another influence in common. Elections are filled with stress for most of those who are directly involved. Problems often arise, and they must be dealt with immediately. Deadlines must be met but volunteer workers are not always available.

Stress can be defined as psychological tension and problems of adjustment. It may come from within the campaign organization itself or from outside sources such as voters, opponents, deadlines, and national events. Stress can potentially disrupt a smooth-running organization. Not much is known about the sources and effects of stress on politicians and political behavior. But a few writers have pointed out that stress is related to politics. Harold Lasswell suggests that various kinds of stress are among the private motives that he believes are displaced onto politics when an individual enters political activity.[17] Robert Lane notes that tensions caused by aggression, sex, and dependency can be sources of political behavior.[18]

Stress on campaigners can have many causes: party leaders who disagree with the campaign's tactics or who hold back financial aid; national events that affect local political opinions, even though the candidate may not have had any connection with these events; conflicts of personality or viewpoints within the campaign staff; demands from voters, active supporters or contributors, or lack of enthusiasm from these quarters. Newspaper readers can find dozens of examples of stress during virtually any well-reported campaign, ranging from late deliveries of bumperstickers to the discovery of men with bugging equipment inside the opposition's headquarters. Perhaps the best explanation of stress in campaigns is that the election is very important to campaigners, but they lack control over its outcome. The election result affects the candidate's ego, but also much more. It determines whether he will be employed in elective office for the coming two or four years, and may also determine the employment of some of his staff members. But the campaigner's efforts are surrounded by unknowns: public opinion is changeable and difficult to measure accurately, and the effectiveness of various campaign techniques is not certain. Reports of campaigns are replete with unexpected events that change the direction of voters' preferences. And as David Leuthold insightfully points out:

The problems of maintaining family relationships, of earning some income, and of campaigning for office combined to place a distinct strain on candidates. Campaigning appeared to be very hard work, whether ringing doorbells or greeting a receiving line, since the candidates were usually striving to establish satisfactory relationships with many different types of people, one right after another.[19]

Do campaigners respond to various kinds of stress in any standardized ways? In particular, do campaigners adapt to the pressures of the election or do they usually try to avoid activities that cause stress? To determine the effects of stress on their behavior, campaigners in Wisconsin were asked, "Is there anything you especially dislike about campaigning?" The number of dislikes they cited was used as an indicator of the amount of stress they felt. This measure cannot accurately describe the intensity of their feelings, since such a description would have required more in-depth psychological testing than was possible during the interview. But in spite of this limitation the question brought out many dimensions of campaigning that cause tension.

The answers to this question were long and colorful, with responses ranging from "nothing" to "everything" (including one from an unhappy manager who stated: "I don't like campaigns at all. I detest politics."). The tallied responses, presented in Table 4-8, show that campaigning produces more stress among managers than among candidates. The candidates may have expressed fewer dislikes because they felt it was politically unwise to find fault with campaigning; since managers are less personally involved, they may have been more inclined to speak freely. But further, candidates do receive more compensation for the long hours they put in, the fatigue, and the voters' demands. Candidates complain about voters, but they also gain reinforcement from the voters who support them. Candidates receive public recognition. Being a candidate for office

Table 4-8
Number of Dislikes Mentioned by Candidates and Managers

Number Mentioned	Candidates	Managers
Two or more dislikes	36%	43%
One dislike only	43	50
No dislikes	21	7
	100%	100%
	N = 28	28

Note: Gamma is −.24.

provides them with status. And being the center of a suspenseful contest can be exciting to the candidate. In contrast, managers must struggle to maintain a volunteer staff without getting the public recognition and status that candidates do. When the campaign meets success, it is the candidate's success rather than the manager's. It is, therefore, not surprising that the managers expressed more dislikes about campaigning, because they appear to get less in return for their time and effort.

Table 4-9 demonstrates that candidates and managers have different kinds of dislikes. Volunteer workers caused the managers the most pressure, followed by demands on their time and energy. Among candidates, time and travel were by far the greatest strain, followed by problems with voters. It is interesting that stress is associated with the areas of campaigning for which each takes primary

Table 4-9
Kinds of Dislikes Mentioned by Candidates and Managers

Dislikes Dealing With	Candidates	Managers
Structure: time, travel, fatigue	57%	36%
Voters	32	21
Campaign workers and volunteers	14	39
Fund-raising	18	21
Opponents	11	4
Other[a]	0	25
No dislikes at all	21	7
	153%[b]	153%[b]

[a]The "other" category included two general comments about the hectic nature of the campaign, a comment from a manager who disliked compromise and another from a manager who disliked campaigning in general, one objection to the need for total commitment to someone else, and a complaint that the campaign's burdens were not distributed equally. One manager only discussed his candidate's dislikes.

[b]Multiple responses were permitted, so percentages total more than 100%.

responsibility: for candidates, the voters and the long hours; for managers, the campaign staff. One might expect that someone who chooses to be a candidate would enjoy contact with voters, and someone who opts for organizing a campaign staff would enjoy working with volunteers. While this may be true, these duties do create day-to-day pressure for the campaigners.

The range of expressed dislikes was enormous. Here are some excerpts:

The manager of a challenger said:
It's kind of like walking around with your hand in someone else's pocket. It's like asking for a loan. Especially in the Democratic party you're constantly aware that you have to continually ask people for contributions who really can't afford it.

Another challenger's manager:
The first [dislike] is voter apathy. I would very much rather deal with people who disagree with me, who will stand up and say, "Yes, I'm voting and I'm voting for your opponent" than with people who say, "Oh, it just doesn't affect me." . . . The second is, those who have never been in politics before find the kind of personal attacks against the candidate very difficult to deal with. . . . If you've been in political campaigns before, I guess you get used to it and say, "Oh well, everyone can't love me," but you can get very strenuously exasperated at the personal kinds of attacks that are made.

The manager of a challenger points out:
Campaigning is probably one of the most grueling things any individual can do. It can be a great ego-booster, but at the same time it can be a great ego-destroyer. People don't know you when you go out into an area, they throw your literature on the ground, things like that.

Another challenger lamented:
The apathy of these people. You know, here I am, trying to go to them, these ass-hole women. I go to their doors. "I'm [John Doe], I'm running for U.S. Congress." You know, I'd be quite honored if a candidate for United States Congress came to *my* door. And they look at me [with blank stares]. I go away, smile, say, "I really feel sorry for you, lady, because everything—the problems you have, is your own fault." . . . They say, "Oh, you're a politician," when here I—I really believe in social change and trying to use the system.

The manager of an incumbent:
Probably the efficiency. That is, if you compare the efficiency in a campaign with the efficiency you'd expect to achieve in a business, I'd say you're lucky if you achieve 25 or 30 percent. . . . You're working with volunteer workers who may or may not do what you'd like done, or may or may not do even what they *say* they'll get done. . . . so the best-laid plans often go astray.

Another manager of an incumbent:
Frequently it's difficult for me to—despite the desirability of getting down with the people—perhaps my choice of words there is significant (and I hope this will be held totally confidential), but I sometimes find it difficult to crank up to getting chatty on the questions that people here are consumed by—you know.

Finally, an incumbent stated:

Well, I dislike the fact that I can't be with my family as much as I'd like to be. . . . Secondly is, of course, there are always people who have many bright ideas, and it's bright to them, but it doesn't fit into the pattern, or it's something which is way out, and you have to handle it diplomatically without hurting them. . . . You don't say some things you'd really *like* to say!

Some patterns can be seen in the campaigners' responses. In particular, challengers express more strain than incumbents do. (Gammas are .44 for candidates, .50 for managers.) The campaign situation is more hostile to challengers. They have more difficulty recruiting competent workers, raising funds, convincing party leaders to support them, and gaining expertise on issues and voters' opinions.

The effects of this unfriendly situation are well described by David Leuthold:

The effort to be competitive produced psychological strain. Candidates agreed that personal contact was the most successful means of influencing voters, but it also appeared that it was the most difficult campaign activity. This was especially true of personal contact with the relatively apathetic voters who were reached only in their homes rather than at a political meeting. Most challengers felt that they needed to ring doorbells in order to have a chance of being elected, while most sure winners and their workers avoided such activity if they possibly could. Workers for sure winners were less likely than workers for competitive candidates or sure losers to have been involved in getting out the vote, registering voters, going door to door, or telephoning—all psychologically difficult tasks. They were more likely, however, to have been involved in such psychologically easy tasks as getting out a mailing or arranging meetings at which their candidate would speak.[20]

The challengers in Wisconsin were also more likely to be involved in close personal contact with voters and volunteers. And this contact did produce more strain. When respondents' dislikes were classified as involving people (voters, supporters, one's opponent, contributors) or structure (time, travel, disorganization, the election process), or both, we find that challengers, in addition to having more dislikes, expressed more people problems than incumbents did (see Table 4-10).[d]

The differences in dislikes of the incumbents and the challengers, as shown in Table 4-10, can also be explained by the kinds of compensations that they each receive when campaigning. Incumbents attract press coverage. Their campaign is likely to be treated with respect because they have been elected in the past and probably will be again. If an incumbent wanders out into the public, he will meet people who have voted for him before. A challenger, on the other hand,

---

[d]There is a positive relationship between the amount of stress and its source. Those with more dislikes were more likely to have people-related rather than structural problems (gammas are .37 for candidates, .48 for managers). This might mean that people-related problems are more numerous, or that campaigners who have these problems are less well-equipped for campaigning that requires extensive personal contact.

Table 4-10
Kinds of Dislikes and Incumbency

Dislikes	Candidates		Managers	
	Incumbents	Challengers	Incumbents	Challengers
People problems	22%	23%	38%	67%
Both kinds of problems	22	46	25	17
Structural problems	56	31	38	17
	100%	100%	101%	101%
	N = 9	13	8	18

Note: Gamma is $-.29$ for candidates, $-.48$ for managers.

cannot depend on his name or his status to attract attention. It is harder for him to get press coverage because he is speaking simply as a candidate, not as a policy-maker. So he must canvass, walk into large crowds, interrupt people going about their daily business, and explain that he is seeking the office of another politician. This is a difficult part to play. Personal contact activities are both more necessary and more difficult for a challenger than an incumbent.

Even when incumbency is held constant, those who would later lose the election expressed more dislikes than the winners-to-be did. Further, the would-be losers' dislikes were weighted toward problems with people, while the prospective winners had more difficulty with structural problems. (The gammas relating the election result and the number of expressed dislikes are .59 for candidates and .64 for managers. The relationships between the election result and the *kinds* of dislikes mentioned are .29 for candidates and .67 for managers.) It is likely that the losing nature of a campaign becomes apparent early and produces tension. However, the reverse might also be true: people who are less comfortable dealing with voters, supporters, and contributors may be less likely to win.

Campaigners expressing more dislikes are more likely to say that campaigning does not have a lot of impact on the election result. Again these attitudes reinforce one another. If a campaigner feels that none of his efforts have much effect on the election outcome, especially if he is an underdog, the pressure on him increases. And as that stress increases, he may look for a rationalization that absolves him of responsibility. If the odds against him are too high and he has no way to affect the outcome, he can say that he should not bear much blame if he loses.[21] In short, the campaigner's chances of winning have a great deal to do with the amount of stress he feels. Having to search for support, especially if the advantages of incumbency are lacking, can be hard on a candidate or manager.

Effects of Stress

Stress in campaigns might produce two kinds of responses. Campaigners might try to adapt to their dislikes while maintaining a heavy schedule, or they might reduce their involvement in the activities they dislike. Generally in the Wisconsin races, campaigners with more dislikes *did* run less extensive and less expensive campaigns. The tendency to avoid stress was strengthened when the stress came from volunteer workers. Stress coming from within the organization, then, is more likely to disable campaigners (and especially managers) than when the stress comes from voters, contributors, or opponents.

The finding that stress is associated with reduced levels of campaigning can be interpreted in two ways. First, campaigners do seem to avoid the activities they dislike. As a veteran congressman states:

I confess I'm—there are some of my colleagues, I won't name them, who year in and year out can generate the same amount of enthusiasm for campaigns, in fact campaign *all* the time and—just fantastic in terms of stamina, interest in doing things by rote over and over again. I'm not quite of that frame of mind and having run eight times, every other year—I have difficulty becoming as enthusiastic about getting into campaigns as I once did years back. I guess very often it is the case that you learn by virtue of past campaigns. Normally you can learn enough so you know what is necessary to do, what is *not* necessary to do. [It is] necessary for me to go to [a factory] plant gate at 5:30 in the morning, so I do that and I *will* do that this time. On the other hand, I'll probably learn that some factories I went to several years back are very small factories and everybody left by six different doors and it didn't pay for me to go to the factory at all. . . . You learn to economize. You learn with less effort to campaign just as effectively as you did before. And this is one compensating fact for, say, declining enthusiasm.

It is hard to imagine *anyone* adapting to plant gates at 5:30 in the morning. However, as this candidate indicates, other campaign activities are also cut back as the experienced candidate or manager finds ways to eliminate or deal with those he finds unpleasant. Second, low levels of campaigning can indicate an undernourished campaign budget, which itself can cause stress.

How does the nature of the stress affect campaigners' responses? Those who expressed voter- or contributor-related problems were much more likely to maintain an active campaign than were respondents who expressed problems with volunteers or structure. In particular, candidates whose problems related to people were likely to use a lot of campaign methods and to have a large budget. They were *not* more likely to turn to the impersonal mass media. They did not shy away from personal contact, even though it was stressful for them. It is interesting, however, that when candidates were asked after the election whether they would have used more canvassing and personal appearances (if funds had been available), those with people problems were much *less* likely than other candidates to say they would have used more of these methods. These pressured candidates could adapt to personal contact *during* the campaign, but from the relative quiet of the post-election period they would not choose to test their adaptability further.

Candidates with people problems were also likely to use polls and other methods of learning public opinion. (Stressed managers were not.) In general, campaigners (especially candidates) tend to adapt to pressure from voters and contributors during the election period. On the other hand, when their dislikes are related to the campaign's volunteer workers, respondents (particularly managers, who have more direct contact with the volunteers) are more likely to cut down on their campaigning. For example, managers who felt pressured by the volunteers were unwilling to say they would expand the campaign's personal contact activities (personal appearances and canvassing) even if the funds were available.

Voters and contributors are vital to a campaign. The pressures they put on candidates and managers, it seems, are considered acceptable. Campaigners adapt to these pressures and maintain personal contact activities, but stress from the campaign volunteers is not accepted as easily. It tends to be associated with less campaign effort, particularly when this stress is felt by managers. Too few workers or unreliable volunteers can sap the campaigner's energy, forcing him to spend time rounding up help rather than rounding up votes.

The problems that volunteers can cause in a campaign again demonstrate that campaigns are social systems, not fighting units. Power in the campaign is diffused, just as in the political party organizations described by Samuel Eldersveld in Wayne County, Michigan. Eldersveld calls the party organization a *stratarchy*, having a series of layers without strong central control. Those in positions of highest authority cannot dominate the others, he points out, because the top power-holders need the support of workers in other strata. Rather than a command structure, a party organization is described as a system of reciprocal deference.[22]

This description also applies to many campaign organizations. Although the candidate can be considered the top power-holder of the campaign, his control over the staff and supporters is often limited. Managers have a sphere of authority different from the candidates'. And both depend on the volunteers and contributors. Without workers and funds, a campaign might as well fold. Since contributions of time and money are voluntary and generally do not bring tangible reward (although there have been notable exceptions), campaigners must work hard to maintain the loyalty of these "underlings." Reciprocal deference is necessary to keep the campaign going. Although most campaigns are not large enough to contain several strata, the ideas discussed by Eldersveld help in understanding the organization of many campaigns.

Reciprocal deference implies that party leaders cannot have complete control over their workers. In campaigns, this lack of control seems to be a major source of pressure on many candidates and managers. Those who were better able to predict the course of their campaigns expressed less strain. Incumbents, experienced at running a successful organization, were less stressed than challengers. Respondents who used traditional campaign methods expressed fewer dislikes than did those who made changes. Candidates whose organization was run formally, with a clear chain of command, were less stressed. (Gammas for the relationship between dislikes and the use of traditional methods are .50 for candidates and .42 for managers. The strength of the association is due in part to the effects of incumbency. Gamma relating candidates' dislikes with formal organization is .36; no relationship is found among managers.) In contrast, informally-run campaigns were associated with voter and volunteer problems. While the independence of various elements of the campaign encourages internal democracy, it also exacts a price from campaign leaders in the form of tension and stress.

Summary and Conclusions

This chapter has investigated some general beliefs that might help organize a campaign and some forces that put pressure on campaign organization. Two beliefs were found to be widely accepted by both candidates and managers. Because the level of agreement on these principles was very high, they can be considered *general norms* of campaigning. First, the campaign's main goal should be to elect the candidate, not to educate the voters. Second, mudslinging (or being caught at mudslinging) is not a proper campaign activity. These two rules are very basic. When other potential norms were tested, agreement among the campaigners decreased. Managers did agree strongly on several other principles of campaigning, but these high levels of agreement were not matched by the candidates. In short, campaigning is not guided by a large number of general principles that are widely accepted by the participants. There are many different viewpoints. Some of these differences are due to variations in the characteristics of constituencies—in some areas the candidate's image may be vitally important to voters, while party labels may guide most voters in other areas.

Three other factors also account for this lack of agreement on basic principles: (1) the influence of campaigners' personalities on their beliefs and activities prevents the development of standardized campaign principles; (2) campaigners' previous experiences, including their occupational background and their past election victories or defeats, affect their beliefs about campaigning; and (3) there are few activities that are considered sure to result in victory at the polls, in the views of most campaigners. Since we have seen that most respondents were mainly concerned with winning, they would have taken seriously any proven link between a particular campaign activity and winning or losing the election. In fact, the two general norms described here *are* clearly associated by campaigners with the election result. Most campaigners believe that people who run for office in order to educate voters are bound to lose, and so are candidates caught using mudslinging tactics. Other general principles about campaigning are *not* widely associated with victory or defeat and therefore, do not have the force of general norms.

But campaigners include many different subgroups, as Chapter 5 will show. These subgroups (candidates and managers, incumbents and challengers, Democrats and Republicans) differ from one another in their attitudes and activities. So there may be *specific* norms that apply to the challengers but not the incumbents, or the managers but not the candidates.

The lack of an elaborate set of general norms has interesting consequences. If there are no sure and standard rules for a successful campaign, then campaigners must rely on their own tested practices or those of others. Without clear guidelines to follow, people who have previously won office are probably motivated to keep doing whatever they did in past winning campaigns. Traditionalism in campaigning may actually stem from the lack of strong campaign norms, just as one could also imagine traditionalism resulting from the existence of strong norms. In contrast, newcomers to campaigning do not have past successes to repeat and must try to find an effective pattern of their own—a difficult job for anyone trying to round up resources at the same time.

Stresses and pressures also affect the running of campaigns. In general when a campaigner expresses more dislikes about campaigning, he tends to be less active, engaging in fewer personal contact activities and less information-seeking. Challengers and campaign managers are especially affected by stress. Candidates, on the other hand, are more likely to adapt to the sources of stress and to continue active campaigning. Perhaps this happens because candidates cannot avoid activities like personal appearances and canvassing, as managers can. They must adapt or the campaign as a whole would suffer. While they may express their irritation, candidates more than managers believe that stress is to be expected in campaigns and it must be accepted.

The source of stress makes a difference in its effects. Campaigners tend to adapt to stress from the voters and contributors. Those who have problems involving volunteer workers have more difficulty and are likely to decrease their campaigning, particularly personal contact activities. The pressures from volunteers are especially felt by managers. Volunteer problems may limit campaign activity for at least two reasons. First, they may force a campaign to expend a lot of time and energy internally, since it must solve the problems created by a lack of manpower or inadequate effort by volunteers, rather than concentrate on influencing voters. Second, the campaign activity may be limited by the reactions of the candidates and managers. Since politicians are accustomed to dealing with politically active people, unwilling volunteers may cause them more irritation on a daily basis than other kinds of problems do.

Again we have seen clear differences between the candidates' and managers' orientations. Candidates feel pressured mainly by the voters and the amount of time and energy required. Pressure on managers comes largely from the volunteers. A campaigner's area of specialization also provides the greatest pressure on his campaign outlook.

One of the most important points about campaign organization as seen so far is that it is characterized by reciprocal deference, just as political parties are. Candidates and managers have separable areas of activity and they need one another. They also need supporters and contributors. But these supporters cannot be expected to give their time, money and energy unless they receive something in return. Campaigners must be able to give these groups a sense of being where the action is, specific favors, emotional reinforcement, or some other kind of reward. The campaign organization must also be prepared to work for the loyalty and interest of the voters. These efforts to win the allegiance of independent groups are often accompanied by stress. Yet we have seen that there are few generally-accepted rules for winning voters and supporters. Therefore we must examine the possibility of specialized rules that apply to subgroups rather than to campaigners in general. The existence of these specialized patterns will be tested in the next chapter.

5 Influences on the Roles Campaigners Play

We have been looking at the campaign organization as a socio-political system. By examining the general norms held by campaigners and the pressures they face, we have been able to observe some patterns of influence on their decision-making. Although few *general* norms were found, there may be *specific* norms that apply to particular campaign roles. We are now in a position to look further into the structure of campaign interactions by determining the roles that campaigners play.

Since this description of campaigns reports, as much as possible, the views of the campaigners themselves, we will be looking at their *role cognitions*—how the campaigners themselves describe their tasks and behavior. The concept of role cognitions is important for students of politics. It provides a link between the individual and the group. Understanding an individual's perceptions of his role helps to define his relationship with other actors in the same system of interactions.[1]

But exactly what is a role? The concept has been widely used in the social sciences, and like many other useful ideas it has been interpreted in many different ways. Roles can be defined as:

... clusters of norms providing for a division of labor or specialization of functions among the members of a group. A person is said to occupy a particular role when, in relation to some special social or task area, the norms applicable to his behavior are different from those applicable to [others].[2]

Then a role is a pattern of expectations and behaviors associated with an actor when he is involved in a particular relationship to the group's communications or activities.

Just as an actor's role is only a part of his total daily behavior, people who take part in campaigns also play other roles. And within the campaign itself, an individual may play only a single role or a large number of roles. For example, a campaign member may participate only in the money-raising effort of the campaign. He may simply contact potential contributors without having any further contact with the candidate or the campaign staff. A more involved campaigner may do many kinds of jobs. On a given day, an active campaign member may begin by joining other staffers for a briefing on the campaign's progress. He may interact with other staff members in some characteristic way. He may typically try to buoy up their confidence with encouraging remarks. He may take the lead in organizing the day's activities, or he may generally suggest changes in campaign plans. His role in relation to the staff could then be described as promoting morale, leading, or innovating.

Next he might be found in conference with a local party leader. Perhaps he tries to smooth out communication problems with the party organization. Now he is playing a second role—that of facilitating relationships with the party. After lunch his schedule calls for meeting with a group of constituents who have volunteered to canvass their neighborhoods for the candidate. This task is very different from his other roles. These volunteers all have different perspectives. They have not dedicated months of their lives to the campaign. Perhaps they need convincing that canvassing is important enough to require several days of their time. Some may have become involved because they feel strongly about a particular issue. They may need persuading that the purpose of the canvass is to elect the candidate, not to communicate their views on that issue. Some may need to be told that they must not include in their spiel some free advertising for another politician. Because the concerns of these volunteers are different from those of party leaders and campaign staffers, the staff member relates to them differently. He will probably tell them about the goals of the campaign, try to maintain their enthusiasm, and get them organized to perform effectively.

Even when he returns home that day he may find himself playing another campaign role. When neighbors ask how the campaign is going, they are not interested in details that a party leader might need to know. Neighbors may express interest in what the candidate is really like and what his chances of victory are. The campaign member, who may have anguished over staffing problems earlier in the day, may want to portray the campaign as unified, hopeful, and dedicated to the candidate when talking with these voters.

An individual, in short, can play many roles in a campaign. These roles can be described in many ways: the number of roles in the campaigner's repertoire, the amount of time and effort he puts into each role, his skills for that role, and his conceptions of the scope and clarity of the role's demands.[3] By examining the roles campaigners play, we are looking at their responses to their environment and to the network of interactions that make up the campaign.

How do we decide what roles a campaigner plays? Some writers have inferred a person's roles by observing his behavior when he deals with various groups of people and then classifying his actions and reactions. Others have asked people in contact with the campaigner for their expectations about his behavior.[4] The most common method, however, is to ask the subject himself. For example, in a study of precinct leaders in North Carolina and Massachusetts, two political scientists operationally defined roles as the activities that these precinct leaders regarded as part of their party job.[5] The leaders were asked whether they performed certain kinds of activities such as canvassing, raising funds, distributing literature, and others. Their responses were then classified according to whether they were primarily campaign-oriented or organization-oriented. Roger

Davidson, in a sample survey of U.S. congressmen, also studied role perceptions by using open-ended questions that asked congressmen to describe their jobs and their problems.[6]

The responses obtained in such surveys are usually classified into several preconceived dimensions of role orientations. Each dimension is meant to show the politician as he responds to different sets of actors or tasks. For example, the commonly-used dimension of *purposive* roles has to do with the substantive purposes of the legislative body or party or campaign.[7] A member of Congress, for instance, could be classified as primarily oriented toward legislative research and debate, or toward the casework he does for his constituents. Another commonly used dimension has to do with *representation*—what or whom the member feels he represents. Representational roles include the instructed delegate and the trustee who follows his own conscience. Representational roles can also be used to separate the nationally-oriented leader from the representative whose primary concern is his own district.[8]

These classifications can provide a great deal of information about the functioning of campaigns. But it must be remembered that a role cognition is "a predisposition to behave in certain ways," not an observation of actual behavior.[9] This implies that self-perceptions do not always correspond with reality. In the Massachusetts-North Carolina study, the authors found that those leaders whose answers were classified as campaign-oriented were not much more likely to perform campaign activities than were the other respondents.[10] This calls for caution in interpreting role cognitions. They simply represent campaigners' own beliefs about their roles.

A further caution is required. Students of political behavior usually fit politicians' responses into certain categories of roles, such as the categories mentioned above. Few campaigners refer to themselves as "delegates" or "trustees," and in fact if those roles were defined to them, they might not agree with the classifications to which they were assigned. There certainly is virtue in clarifying ideas that the respondent cannot articulate himself. But it is important to avoid distorting the respondent's perceptions in order to make them fit certain categories. Important information could be overlooked because it does not fit into the preconceived pattern.

The preceding three chapters have presented many different relationships among campaigners' attitudes and behavior. Their responses can be viewed as a kind of mass answer to the question, "What tasks do you perform in the campaign, and how do you view campaigning?" Having examined the responses, it is now possible to draw out several role dimensions. These role dimensions are not exhaustive; rather, they reflect the areas of campaigning that this study was designed to explore. The data do not tell which of these dimensions are regarded as most important, because the campaigners were not asked to rank-order their tasks. But a broad range of tasks and attitudes has been uncovered and certain patterns have appeared.

Three role dimensions are especially clear. In order to compare these data with other research, the role dimensions can be defined as representational and purposive. Within each role dimension two roles have been described. I intend, however, to present enough data so that the reader can draw his or her own conclusions about the fitness of these classifications.

First, there are many different ways to define representation.[11] It is defined in this book as the interaction of demands and influence between leaders and constituents, requiring open channels of communication between them. Defining representation in this way enables us to see it as a process rather than as an end result. We have seen that campaigners differ in the extent to which they seek voters' opinions about issues, the extent to which they use polls and other relatively reliable methods of learning voters' views, and the extent to which they listen to party leaders, newspapermen, and contributors. Campaigners who make an effort to learn constituents' views will be termed delegates, those who do not will be called trustees.

Second, patterns have also been found in the campaigners' feelings about making changes in the campaign. Since these feelings have to do with their style of campaigning and their mission as campaigners, they constitute a purposive role relating to campaign *style*. Six measures of change-related attitudes and behavior are relevant to this role dimension. Chapter 3 discussed two measures of behavior regarding change (in methods and workers) and three measures of attitudes having to do with changes in the campaign. Respondents were also asked whether they feel their campaign is organized formally (with a strict chain of command and clearly defined jobs) or informally. Running an informal campaign tends to be related to flexibility, but these two items do not overlap completely. Within this role dimension (termed here the *style* of campaigning), role cognitions will be classified as innovative or traditional.

The third role dimension relates to the *focus* of campaign activity. Two kinds of data are involved here. Campaigners can be grouped according to the main concern of their activities: the volunteers and others within the organization, or the voters and other outside groups. Campaigners also divide into those primarily oriented toward the mass media and "remote" campaign methods, and those mainly oriented toward direct personal contact with the voters. Together these measures describe whether a campaigner directs his activities largely toward the campaign organization or toward the voters. The campaigner's *focus* will be classified as voter-oriented or organization-oriented. The distribution of candidates and managers on all three role dimensions is shown in Table 5-1.

A fourth role dimension discussed by other writers involves the generally accepted folkways of many organizations. Davidson refers to these as *consensual roles*.[12] Not many generally accepted folkways were found among these campaigners, but at times the respondents' theories of campaigning provide interesting information about their roles. Wherever these responses increase our understanding of role cognitions, they will be reported.

Table 5-1
Role Orientations of Candidates and Managers

	Candidates	Managers
I. *Representational Roles*		
Makes an effort to learn voters' views on issues	68%	55%
Reports talking with voters about issues	71	48
Asks party leaders about the campaign	75	63
Asks newspapermen about the campaign	38	60
II. *Purposive Roles—Style*		
Uses different methods in 1970	15	30
Uses new personnel in 1970	48	37
Willing to make campaign changes	33	46
Willing to make changes, in retrospect	72	65
Prefers at least some flexibility for candidate	72	82
Prefers an informal organization	19	46
III. *Purposive Roles—Focus*		
Considers media more important than personal appearances	19	39
Uses a lot of personal appearances	89	72
Uses a lot of canvassing	38	33
Expresses problems with voters	32	21
Expresses problems with volunteers or organization	14	39
Takes opponent's plans into account	54	34
Spends half or more time planning rather than campaigning	11	48

Note: Again it is necessary to point out that even within the same campaign, candidates and managers can disagree even on questions such as whether "a lot" or "some" canvassing was used.

Some influences on these role dimensions have already helped to fill out their content. In Chapter 2 it was demonstrated that uncertain campaigners are more likely than assured campaigners to seek out voters' views on issues and to use polls and canvassing. Uncertain campaigners, then, are more likely to be delegates than trustees. They seem to believe that keeping open lines of communication with voters may help improve their chances of victory.

Uncertain campaigners are also more likely to be innovators rather than traditionalists. This is also true of challengers rather than incumbents. So innovation is also stimulated when a campaigner does not feel sure of winning the election. And, especially among candidates, innovation is associated with a personality trait—tolerance of ambiguity.

But the full picture of relationships with these role dimensions has not yet been painted. Does the campaigner's position in the campaign, his party, his occupation, or the type of office he seeks have any impact on the purposive and representational roles he assumes? By relating components of the role dimensions to these independent variables, we can learn much more about the nature of the roles. The results may also show the extent to which different roles are clearly defined by the campaigners who play them.

Independent Variables

In order to determine the influence of one of these variables on role cognitions, it must be established that associations among the independent variables are low. Otherwise, if two variables are strongly related and the population is small, it is difficult to separate out the independent effects of each. Table 5-2 presents the interrelationships among these variables, with the exception of occupation.

Two of these relationships are strong and should be kept in mind. Incumbents tended to be found in the congressional races more than in the statewide races, and more among the Republicans than the Democrats in this group of campaigners. In addition, occupation was significantly associated with all four other variables. Looking at the type of election, for example, all the teachers were in congressional campaigns, while lawyers and journalists were somewhat over-represented among statewide campaigners. Regarding position in the campaign, all the political aides were managers, as were all the journalists. On the other hand, most lawyers (69 percent) were candidates, as were most businessmen (59 percent) and teachers (64 percent). Occupational groups having a larger-than-average proportion of incumbents were journalists (67 percent), political aides (62 percent) and lawyers (54 percent). On the other hand, 71 percent of businessmen and 82 percent of teachers were challengers. And with the exception of lawyers, there was a particularly strong association between occupation and party choice. Journalists and teachers were all Democrats, while 88 percent of businessmen and 62 percent of political aides were Republicans.

In short, occupation is so tightly interwoven with the other independent

Table 5-2
Gamma Matrix of Four Independent Variables

	Type of Election	Incumbency	Party
Incumbency	.44	—	—
Party	.02	.62	—
Position (candidate or manager)	.15	.10	.03

variables that it will be difficult to draw firm conclusions about its effects. The patterns of effects that will be presented here must be interpreted with these relationships among independent variables in mind. In general it was found that much of the effect of the type of election was spurious, due to the influence of incumbency. Incumbency also accounts for part of the influence of Republican party affiliation, although party does exert some independent influence. With this in mind, let us examine each factor in detail.

The Influence of Party Affiliation

Differences between the two major parties—whether they exist and in what forms—have long concerned students of politics. The importance of party has been affirmed by writers such as Lewis Froman, who proposes that the setting of the election is crucial, since it limits the support a candidate can gain. The party distribution of voters, he states, is the most important element of the setting.[13] Nelson Polsby and Aaron Wildavsky too imply that party is important when they suggest that the two parties have different goals. Democrats, they write, must aim for a large turnout since the majority of voters identify as Democrats. Republicans, on the other hand, must concentrate on independents and wayward Democrats as well as Republican identifiers. This assumes candidates are "keenly aware" that most votes are determined by party identification.[14] Other writers indicate that party influence over both voters and politicians is waning. Samuel Eldersveld found, for example, that party affiliation did not make much difference in the role perceptions of precinct leaders in Wayne County, Michigan.[15]

Party does have an impact on these campaigners' role perceptions (see Table 5-3). Beginning with representational roles, Democrats were more likely to act as delegates, seeking information about voters' opinions on issues. The parties also differed in the other sources of information they used. While Republicans were more likely to use party leaders as an information source, Democrats were more likely to get issue-oriented cues from contributors. The latter finding supports John Kingdon's point that Democrats in his sample were more likely to say their supporting coalition was backing them for policy rather than personal reasons.[16]

Other researchers studying representational roles have reported different results. Davidson states that the *Republican* congressmen in his sample were more likely to act as instructed delegates than Democrats were.[17] The difference can be reconciled by looking at the direction of party dominance. Samuel Patterson suggests that the minority party is more likely to be campaign-oriented than the dominant party, and less likely to be organization-oriented.[18] In order to overcome the advantages of the dominant party, the minority party must be more energetic in establishing communication with the voters. Therefore the candidates of the disadvantaged party can be expected to consider the delegate

Table 5-3
Effects of Party Affiliation on Role Cognitions

	Democrats	Republicans	Gamma
I. *Representational Roles*			
Makes an effort to learn voters' views on issues	72%	50%	.45
Uses public opinion polls	31	25	.13
Asks party leaders about the campaign	64	74	.23
Sees contributions as dependent on issues	43	15	.37
II. *Purposive Roles–Style*			
Uses different methods in 1970	28	18	.19
Prefers flexibility for candidate	61	25	.60
Has an informal organization	70	41	.57
III. *Purposive Roles–Focus*			
Considers personal appearances more important than media	48	56	.14
Uses no television advertising	52	29	.24
Uses a lot of personal appearances	93	68	.68
Uses a lot of canvassing	46	24	.31
	N = 29	28	

role very seriously. In Davidson's study the Republicans were the minority party in Congress. In this state the Democrats could claim that position. A majority of incumbents were Republicans, even though Wisconsin is a two-party competitive state. Wisconsin Republicans were also more likely to be assured about the election results. (Gammas for this relationship are .30 for candidates and .46 for managers.) In this study too, then, delegate role orientations were more likely to be found in the minority party.

Traditionalists were more likely to be in Republican, not Democratic ranks. Republicans were much more likely to run a formal organization, to avoid flexibility, and slightly more likely to retain the methods used in their last campaign. This is due in part to the influence of incumbency overlapping with Republican affiliation. (Incumbents were quite likely to prefer traditional methods.) Just as Republicans were found to be less tolerant of ambiguity, they were also philosophically and behaviorally less favorable to change than Democrats. Party influence on role cognitions, in short, can take two forms. First, campaigners may be responding to the dominant or minority position of their party. Second, deeper philosophical differences between the parties may have an impact on the roles their members play.

Party also has some influence on the third role dimension. Republicans were more likely to use media such as television, and less likely to use personal appearances and canvassing than Democrats were. This confirms the report of James Perry that Republicans are generally more likely to use New Politics methods than Democrats are.[19] But the respondents' orientations toward voters or volunteers were not clearly affected by their party affiliations.

Briefly, consensual roles also reflect some party influence. In particular, Democrats were more likely than Republicans to target their campaigns at independent voters. (Gammas for this relationship are .32 for candidates and .56 for managers.) This contradicts Polsby and Wildavsky's assumption that Democrats would concentrate on turning out the Democratic faithful. The data also question the authors' suggestion that candidates are "keenly aware" that voters vote their party identification. Among these campaigners the understanding is that image, not party label, determines most voting behavior.

In conclusion, there are clear party differences on at least two of the three role dimensions. Democrats are more likely to choose the delegate role than Republicans are, and they also tend to innovate more. These findings broadly parallel the differences between challengers and incumbents, and in fact more Democrats are challengers than incumbents. But even when incumbency is taken into account, party still has an independent effect on these role cognitions.

Type of Election: Congressional or Statewide

There are two reasons why the type of election might be expected to affect campaigners' role cognitions. First, a congressman's job and environment is quite different from that of a state official. Therefore we might expect that different types of people would be attracted to the two roles. Congressional hopefuls would anticipate being a part of a well-established and self-contained institution. Their attention would be held by legislative work, national issues, relationships with other legislators from around the nation. In contrast, statewide campaigners would look forward to a primarily executive job. Their concerns would involve state policy; their co-workers would share a state perspective. Second, the constituency of a would-be congressman differs in both size and diversity from the statewide constituency. Campaigners for state office must appeal to all segments of the state: city dwellers and farmers, upstate and downstate partisans. Congressional districts, mainly because they are smaller, tend to be more homogeneous in social characteristics and problems.

However, the type of election exerts strong influence on only one of the three roles discussed here (see Table 5-4). Looking at representation, statewide campaigners were more likely than congressional respondents to consult with the voters about issues and to use polls. Their greater concern with voters' opinions is probably due to the high proportion of challengers among statewide hopefuls.

Table 5-4
Effects of Type of Election on Role Cognitions

	Congressional	Statewide	Gamma
I. *Representational Roles*			
Makes an effort to learn voters' views on issues	59%	69%	.22
Uses public opinion polls	24	38	.35
Asks party leaders about the campaign	61	93	.78
II. *Purposive Roles—Style*			
Uses different methods in 1970	21	25	.04
Prefers flexibility for candidate	46	33	.11
Has an informal organization	54	60	.07
III. *Purposive Roles—Focus*			
Considers personal appearances more important than media	62	27	.52
Uses no television advertising	39	44	.12
Uses a lot of personal appearances	78	88	.28
Uses a lot of canvassing	32	44	.04
	N = 41	16	

Challengers may feel they can make up for their lack of established support by seeking more information about voters' preferences. This argument is strengthened by the fact that statewide campaigners were much more uncertain about the election result than were congressional campaigners. (Gammas for this relationship are 1.00 for candidates and .62 for managers.) Statewide respondents were also more likely to use party leaders as a source of information. Perhaps this bears out the contention that the state and county units are considered more vital to the party organization than are the congressional districts.

Table 5-4 shows that there are few clear differences in purposive role orientations between statewide and congressional campaigners. The only finding of interest is that although statewide hopefuls used more personal appearances, they also tended to believe that the mass media were more important to their campaign than was personal contact with the voters. This indicates that persons running for state office use a broad range of techniques to impress the voters, primarily because these persons are largely challengers and result-uncertain.

In general, then, the type of election has not fulfilled expectations that it would make a difference in campaigners' decision-making. Its effects are felt only in representational roles, with statewide campaigners more inclined to seek information from voters. Even this association seems to be due to the needs of statewide challengers. Therefore, because the pattern of results is not very clear or consistent, it seems that the type of election is not as powerful an influence on role cognitions as is party identification.

Campaigners' Occupations

Occupational experiences can influence a person's views on life, including his political views. Studies of voting behavior have found that considerable change can take place in party identification and political orientation during young adulthood, when most people begin marriage and a career.[20] The daily influence of co-workers and family can reinforce certain kinds of political attitudes. This reinforcement increases with advancing age. An individual's environment becomes more and more homogeneous with respect to political and social beliefs.

Much has been written about the political activity of certain occupational groups, such as lawyers.[21] And familiar stereotypes portray the conservative businessman, the radical college professor, the skeptical journalist. The Wisconsin campaigners included occupational groups that might differ in political behavior: businessmen (N = 17), lawyers (N = 13), teachers, primarily at the college level (N = 11), journalists (N = 3) and political aides (N = 8).[a]

In fact, occupation affected these campaigners' role cognitions. It is necessary to remember, however, that the sizes of the individual occupational groups are very small and that other variables overlap with occupation and may account for part or all of these relationships. To avoid a false impression of significance, the percentages and measures of association are not presented in tabular form.

Lawyers tended to seek voters' views on issues more than any other occupational group did. Lawyers also used more methods of campaigning than other groups. Among lawyers, 92 percent used at least six of the seven methods rated, while journalists and businessmen were least active in persuading voters and seeking voters' views. Lawyers may have been more energetic because they were least assured about the election result, while journalists and political aides were the most assured. Or it may be that lawyers tend to have more of the interpersonal skills needed for political activity, and therefore feel more comfortable with a lot of voter contact than do persons with other occupational skills.[22]

Teachers were second to lawyers in seeking information from the voters. The obvious explanation, that lawyers and teachers are accustomed to talking easily with different kinds of people, is challenged by the low level of information-seeking among journalists, who should also have this skill. But the minimal information-gathering done by journalists probably reflects the fact that two of the three were working for incumbents.

---

[a]Respondents classified as political aides had no other occupation but political activity, and were generally young campaign managers just out of college. Five campaigners were classified as "other": a factory worker, minister, farmer, union official, and fireman.

Looking at innovation-tradition as a role dimension, two groups were consistently found on opposing sides. Teachers tended to be most flexible and willing to change, while businessmen scored lowest on change and innovation. At times, it seems that popular stereotypes may reflect some actual differences in attitudes. Ratings of the other three groups varied according to the measure used. For example, journalists were most likely to favor flexibility in campaigns, but were only slightly more tolerant of ambiguity than businessmen. Lawyers, on the other hand, rejected flexibility as much as the businessmen did, but scored highest on tolerance of ambiguity.

No significant patterns were seen in the effect of occupation on voter- or organization-orientation. But one very interesting finding appeared in campaigners' theories about elections. There was a wide range of opinion about the goal of the campaign. All three journalists and three-quarters of the teachers felt education is a desirable goal for the campaign. On the other hand, fully half of the businessmen disagreed. The businessmen's greater pessimism about the possibility of educating the voters, when combined with their tendency to run less active campaigns, do less information-seeking and avoid change, points to a reluctance to become involved with voters and active politics. This approach to campaigning is very different from that of the teachers and lawyers interviewed.

These occupational groups included many different types of persons. Businessmen-campaigners varied from advertising executives to heads of large and complex corporations to low-level management. Differences in the perspectives of these subgroups is understandable. A much larger group of campaigners would be needed to provide a definitive analysis of the relationships between occupational experiences and campaigning. But in general, clear patterns of behavior have appeared among these different groups. We cannot be sure that these patterns actually reflect the influence of occupation. But the patterns do harmonize well with expectations about the political activity of these different occupational groups. This area should provide interesting and fruitful research in the future.

Incumbency

The clearest influence on campaigners' role cognitions is incumbency. Incumbents think and behave differently from challengers on all of the role dimensions considered here. Incumbents are much less likely to act as delegates, much less innovative, and more inclined toward the use of the mass media rather than face-to-face campaign methods (see Table 5-5).

The powerful effect of incumbency has two causes. First and foremost, incumbents are much more secure in expecting to win than challengers are. Although some writers have suggested that incumbents work just as hard to win as challengers do,[23] incumbents in this study did not match the challengers'

Table 5-5
Effects of Incumbency on Role Cognitions

	Incumbents	Challengers	Gamma
I. *Representational Roles*			
Makes an effort to learn voters' views on issues	57%	65%	.17
Uses public opinion polls	13	38	.56
Asks party leaders about the campaign	78	62	.37
Believes contributors give for issue reasons	26	75	.74
II. *Purposive Roles–Style*			
Uses different methods in 1970	5	44	.71
Willing to make campaign changes	23	52	.51
Willing to make changes, in retrospect	47	81	.66
Prefers flexibility for candidate	39	45	.24
Has an informal organization	41	66	.47
III. *Purposive Roles–Focus*			
Considers personal appearances more important than media	62	45	.38
Uses no television advertising	26	50	.19
Uses a lot of personal appearances	70	88	.50
Uses a lot of canvassing	10	52	.51
Expresses problems with voters	29	42	*
Expresses problems with volunteers or organization	29	38	*
	N = 23	34	

*Gammas were not calculated because the number of campaigners choosing each of these categories was too small for gammas to be meaningful.

efforts. They had already done the hard work of establishing their credentials in earlier campaigns; most could now afford to take it easy. Further, in addition to the many other advantages an incumbent has over other candidates, he is also likely to have a strong vote-getting appeal on his own, even without the status of incumbent.[24]

It is interesting that while incumbents were generally more assured about victory than challengers were, the managers of incumbents were even more assured than the incumbents themselves. Perhaps managers, who are one step removed from the front lines, are better able to maintain their confidence in the campaign than if they were out meeting the voters.

The second big difference between incumbents and challengers is that the campaign is not the incumbent's only shot at political activity. Incumbents are in contact with the voters throughout their two- or four-year term. Challengers usually have only the period between August and election day to make their mark. Charles Clapp reports that the congressmen he interviewed agreed that non-election years were the most effective for strengthening their support.[25] And the incumbents in this study were much less likely than challengers to feel that the campaign period was important to their election. (Gammas for this relationship are .39 for candidates, .60 for managers.) As one incumbent's manager stated:

I think it's a mistake to think of the campaign as a specified period of four or five or however many weeks or months. To a real political animal, he's campaigning all the time. Every letter that we write to every individual, every appearance the congressman makes, every newsletter and a whole variety of other contacts of that form, are a campaign effort. Not in a crass sense, but in the sense that they reflect the man. . . .

The campaign environment is quite different for an incumbent than for a challenger. An incumbent brings to the campaign his experiences in office and the contacts, information, and assurance he has gained during his term. He comes back to a constituency that has already chosen him as their representative. He has already put together a successful organization, and many of his former volunteers may be willing to work to elect him again.

Incumbents, however, may at times be handicapped by their experience. After many terms in office, their age may be used against them. Incumbent vice presidents seeking to win the presidency may have a particularly difficult job. They must defend the record of the past administration even though they may not have had much to say about its policies. But the constituents of most incumbent congressmen and most state officials are not likely to know much about their record in office. In balance, incumbency is generally a definite advantage without many drawbacks.

Table 5-5 shows that incumbents are less likely to choose the role of delegate than challengers are. Incumbents do not seek as much information about voters' preferences. We might assume that incumbents feel they get enough information from their office mail and from district visits. But their trustee orientation may have another source. Clapp reports that most congressmen in his sample did very little information-gathering because they felt that voters have very little information.[26] Experience teaches the incumbent that he has little to gain from seeking out voters' views, although he has a lot to gain from proclaiming that this is a proper thing to do.

Perhaps the best explanation of incumbents' preference for the trustee role is that they do not *need* to act as delegates. The role of delegate is not an easy one. A delegate tries to seek out constituents' opinions, but a large number of constituents are apathetic and uninformed. Tracking down public opinion takes a good deal of energy and time. Those who are vulnerable to defeat can help themselves by performing this task. But without the spur of vulnerability, most incumbents are not motivated to actively seek out voters' views.[27]

One of the most striking findings is that incumbents are much less accepting of change than challengers are, as was discussed in Chapter 2. Incumbents and challengers do not differ in their tolerance of ambiguity. Therefore these results do not indicate a deep-seated "incumbent personality" that resists change. The response is more pragmatic. Past success molds current practice.

This lack of appreciation for a flexible, innovative campaign has several causes. Some incumbents see their style of campaigning as a trademark, a pattern of communication with the voters just like the habitual ways people greet acquaintances or write their name. Of course, many voters may not have the foggiest notion what an incumbent's trademark is, and may not even care. But if an incumbent feels that people identify him with certain methods, he will probably be reluctant to experiment. Alternatively, incumbents may see just enough uncertainty in politics to make them cling to techniques they associate with victory. Or perhaps candidates who stay with traditional and highly organized styles of campaigning make a better impression on the voters and are more likely to remain incumbents.

On the innovator-traditionalist dimension, in short, incumbents come down soundly on the side of tradition. But looking at the third role dimension, the results are more complex. Incumbents are more likely to use remote methods of campaigning such as television, and less likely to use face-to-face methods like canvassing and personal appearances. In the same vein, Chapter 2 reported that increasing assurance about the election result is linked with greater use of the efficient, but also remote, mass media and less use of face-to-face campaigning.

But when asked whether the media are more important to their campaigns than personal appearances are, most of the incumbents said no. If personal appearances are more important, why do incumbents use fewer personal appearances than challengers do? The duties of office often keep incumbents away from the campaign until shortly before the election. Some incumbents want to use more personal appearances but simply cannot find the time. Others are grateful that there is not enough time to campaign extensively. The mass media cost less in time and energy. But most incumbents also know that they must express their delight at meeting voters, even if they actually avoid such activity at all costs.

Contrary to much political folklore, incumbents are more likely than challengers to say that educating the voters is feasible and desirable in a campaign. (Gammas for this relationship are .33 for candidates, .30 for managers.) This may seem surprising, since "educational campaigns" are generally thought to be conducted by people who expect to lose. But except for guaranteed sacrifice candidates (there are a few in this study who did not accept their fate), it is the incumbents who can afford the time spent educating the voters, since they are more assured of winning. Again, however, incumbents may opt for education not because they plan to behave accordingly, but because they believe they should express the "democratic" response to a question. Challengers, on the other hand, are frank; they often learn the wry lesson that educating the voters about issues is done at the candidate's expense. As one challenger's manager pointed out:

You don't win an election by educating. If we wanted to be satisfied with what everybody's come to call a moral victory, we could try educating, but the issues are too complex. All it takes is for [the opponent] to get up and say, "You don't understand the technicalities of the vote," and it destroys everything you've said about the issues.

The profile of these data is clear. Incumbents are more secure in expecting to win, more independent of voters' demands on them, less active in campaigning and information-gathering, and more traditional in approach. Incumbency has a strong impact on campaigners' attitudes and behavior. By simply knowing whether a campaigner is an incumbent or challenger, reasonably accurate predictions can be made about his role cognitions.

Moreover, it appears that the demands of incumbency are much more clearly defined than are the rules governing a challenger's behavior. Incumbents tend to develop a pattern of campaigning that is then repeated. Challengers come into a campaign without a set of proven campaign techniques, at least for winning the office they now seek. Although most challengers say that they want to meet personally with voters and to try new techniques, the appropriate ways to go about these jobs may be difficult to determine. Chapter 4 noted that campaign stress is associated with seeking more information, believing contributors give because of issues, being satisfied with a bare majority rather than a big victory, and trying new campaign methods. It is instructive that all these conditions, as well as greater campaign stress, are more common among challengers. Perhaps this simply means that it is psychologically harder to challenge than to defend, at least at the congressional and state level. But it is also likely that the challenger has fewer landmarks, fewer tested patterns to guide him than the incumbent does.

Erving Goffman points out that an individual in a new role, as most challengers are, does not get many cues about how to conduct himself, "nor will the facts of his new situation press sufficiently on him from the start to determine his conduct without his giving further thought to it."[28] Challengers often mentioned that their predecessor had not left proper records, that they had to experiment with campaign methods to learn which methods would work for them, that they were testing out different attacks on their opponent to see which ones were best received by the voters. An incumbent may have to do some of the same testing if he plans to change his approach to fit the style and weaknesses of each new opponent. But an incumbent's experience in conducting campaigns still provides him with a set of ground rules that the challenger must develop for himself.[29]

Position in the Campaign

Joe McGinniss in *The Selling of the President 1968* reports that during the 1968 campaign Richard Nixon insisted on filming a television spot on a controversial local issue against the advice of his staff. One adviser expressed dismay to another at the decision. The second adviser quietly replied, "That's all right, Len. It'll never get on the air."[30]

Such conflicts between the candidate and his staff, although they often go unreported in order to maintain the appearance of harmony, can be expected in campaigns. The requirements of the two positions are quite different. A candidate must be an unusual type of person. He must believe in something—whether an issue, a party, an ideal of public service, or himself—so strongly that he is personally willing to risk the negative judgment (or possibly the amusement) of thousands of people to achieve it. In the end, he is responsible for the campaign and for the co-workers and friends who give some of their private time to promote him for office. One candidate described his lonely responsibility for the efforts made to elect him:

I'm uneasy about the fact that so many people are involved in the campaign and therefore dependent on me. If I lose this election by two votes, these people have worked an awfully long time for that and I've let them down. That gets to me inside. I lose a lot of sleep because of that kind of thing. It really upsets me. I'm a very independent person. And if I could go out and run this election all on my own—my own money, my own time—then whether I win or lose, then damn it I won or lost. But that's not the way it is now. . . . I go upstairs to bed and think, "What if I lose? What about the guy who sent me a $100 check? How about the girl who gave up x hours of her time?"

In contrast, no matter how committed the manager may be to the goals of the campaign, he has a different perspective. He is not the central figure. His picture does not appear on thousands of brochures and he is not likely to be recognized as a public figure when he walks down the street. If the campaign has even the most basic division of labor, the manager is probably occupied with maintaining the headquarters, the staff and the organization, not meeting the voters.

Relationships among variables may change quite markedly when we take into account the respondent's position in the campaign. For example, the overall association between party identification and the respondent's estimate of the importance of campaigning is negligible: .06. But there are two significant relationships concealed inside. Among candidates, the Republicans are more likely to believe campaigning is important (gamma is .50). Among managers,

Democrats are more likely to feel this way (gamma is .48). How can differences such as these be explained?

The effects of position in the campaign on role cognitions are not as striking as those of incumbency, but they nevertheless produce distinctive patterns (see Table 5-6; percentages can be found in Table 5-1). Candidates tend to take the delegate role with voters and party leaders. For example, while 68 percent of candidates reported talking with voters about issues, only 55 percent of managers did so. Candidates may show more interest in voters' views because they are more uncertain than managers about the election result. Too, candidates are more likely to have contact with voters than managers are, and consequently more opportunity to be exposed to their opinions. On the other hand, managers were more likely to talk with newspapermen about the campaign.

Candidates were also more likely than managers to want a big victory, as opposed to a bare majority of the votes. A big victory would bolster the candidate's ego, his chances for higher office, his standing among his colleagues, and the mandate he wants for his stands on issues. These additional goals, beyond winning office, indicate that the candidate's expectations about the election are broader than those of the manager. Perhaps they also increase the

Table 5-6
Effects of Campaign Position on Role Cognitions: Gamma Associations

Candidates, Compared with Managers, Tend to . . .	Gamma
I. *Representational Roles*	
Make more effort to learn voters' views on issues	.26
Ask party leaders about the campaign more	.28
Ask newspapermen about the campaign *less*	.41
Believe contributions are *not* contingent on issues	.13
Be more result-uncertain	.32
Want a big victory rather than a bare majority	.24
II. *Purposive Roles–Style*	
Use the same methods in 1970 as in previous races	.11
Be less willing to make campaign changes	.13
Prefer a more formal organization	.53
Score *less* tolerant of ambiguity	.21
III. *Purposive Roles–Focus*	
Report use of more personal appearances	.26
Express fewer dislikes about campaigning	.24
Express problems with structure rather than people	.45
Take account of their opponent's plans more	.37

candidate's uncertainty about the election result. They further remind us that the hoped-for result would be the *candidate's* big victory, not the manager's or the staff's.

Candidates are more traditional than managers. These candidates were much more likely to prefer a formally organized campaign, where each person does a specific job and knows his place in the chain of command. Candidates were less tolerant of ambiguity. Although the relationships are not significant, candidates were slightly more likely to retain the methods used in their last campaign and to avoid making changes during the campaign. One possible explanation is that candidates seem to have a greater emotional and physical investment in the campaign. Their personalities are more closely intertwined with their campaigning, and they are more likely to personally identify with particular campaign techniques than managers are. This emotional investment may increase the candidate's conservatism and his reliance on tradition. Managers, in contrast, respond more pragmatically. Characteristic of many managers, one manager of an incumbent stated:

If [a candidate's] got the brains of a jackass he'll keep it flexible. Because if you set up a plan and say this is the way it is, come hell or high water, you're saying people are stupid and you can mold them to your way of thinking. No one can anticipate all things in a campaign. And so you *have* to be flexible.

Finally, it is clear that candidates and managers are oriented toward different areas of campaigning. Although there were few major differences in the two groups' perceptions about the use of different campaign methods, they disagreed when they looked back on method use. When asked what campaign activities they would like to have increased, if funds were available, nearly half of the candidates would consider using more personal appearances; fully 65 percent of managers would not. This echoes earlier findings that candidates consider their personal appearances to be a strong selling point for the campaign.

Several other results add to an understanding of voter- and organization-oriented roles. Although it has been reported that candidates expressed more voter-related dislikes than managers did, when all dislikes are divided into those involving people and structure, only one in four of the candidates' dislikes had to do with people, compared with 58 percent of managers' dislikes. Candidates, in fact, expressed fewer dislikes about campaigning in general than managers did. Candidates seem to adapt to working with large numbers of people with less irritation and strain than the managers do. They seem better able to contain their downswings in mood, without letting these downswings affect their campaign performance. For example, two-thirds of the candidates reported that the campaign organization had activities to bolster the morale of the staff; but only 32 percent of the managers expressed active concern about the candidate's morale. Managers typically commented that the candidate did not show much discouragement or frustration and that his morale did not cause concern among the staff.

Candidates also tended to be more aware of the opposition's activities than managers were. Candidates were more likely than managers to report that they took into account information about the opponent's plans when planning their own activities. Again, dealing with persons outside of the staff and the volunteers is the specialty of the candidate.

So managers as a group are different from candidates as a group. But there are also differences within individual campaigns. For example, only 70 percent of the candidate-manager pairs agreed on the value of educating voters in the campaign. The same proportion of pairs agreed on whether they made an effort to learn voters' views on issues. Sixty-four percent agreed on whether the campaign organization was run formally or informally. When asked whether the campaign *should* be run formally or informally, only 60 percent of candidate-manager pairs agreed. Each of these questions had two possible responses. Therefore, a 50 percent level of agreement would be expected if candidates' and managers' views were distributed at random. The reported levels of candidate-manager agreement within campaigns, then, are not very high.

These disagreements do not mean that an individual candidate and his manager are poles apart. On the question of flexibility, for example, three possible responses were suggested to the campaigners: that they preferred being flexible, partly flexible, or to stick with a previous plan. If candidates' and managers' views were randomly distributed, only 33 percent of the candidate–manager pairs would be expected to agree on the same response. In fact, only 33 percent *did* agree on the same response. But another 59 percent were only one point removed, leaving only 8 percent of the candidate-manager pairs facing each other from opposite ends of the scale. And the fact that these disagreements are reported to an interviewer does not mean that candidates and their managers expressed their points of disagreement to one another. A campaign organization might run in perfect harmony with the candidate believing in a strict master plan and the manager preferring flexibility so long as their preferences remained in the realm of theory. It might even be possible for each to act on his belief in his own area of the campaign without any conflict resulting.

The number of disagreements between candidates and managers, however, is startling. This clearly illustrates the diversity of viewpoints in campaigns. These differences are best expressed by the campaigners themselves:

A challenger candidate points out:
When the majority on your staff are volunteers, sometimes they're more difficult than the opposition. It's very difficult to make your supporters understand that you appreciate their interest but that you can't be all things to all people.

Another challenger draws a clearer picture of differences:
My campaign manager prepared this *beautiful* brochure—well, it's really high

grade—but I say it's a waste of money, because a matchbook would be just as effective for the average voter. . . . I think he's a little wrong in that he has too much faith in the average voter. He thinks they're issue-oriented, I know they're not.

The following two challengers, a candidate and his manager, provide a sharp picture of the differences in their role perspectives:

The candidate says:
My manager wants to push specific issues and I don't agree. I think the issues are going to hurt me more than help me. The candidate is normally emotionally involved, and doesn't want to do this or that; and the manager should be much more open-minded and should have a better analysis of them than the candidate. But in my case this doesn't exist. [My manager] is excellent but he's not doing the campaign the way I would want it done. Of course I may be biased because I'm the candidate and I'd always like to see 100 times more work done than just the normal routine.

The manager, referring to the candidate as "C" and his opponent as "O," points out:
Any campaign manager would like a campaign to be run very formally, very strictly . . . the campaign manager almost has the autocratic power of a dictator during that time. . . . All the candidate does, as far as I'm concerned, and this is my department, he turns his body over to the campaign chairman and his committee and he just follows their direction. You tend to just spin wheels if the candidate gets involved and says, "Look, I don't think I should be doing this, I think I should be doing that." He has to accept direction. . . . I read every newspaper, every word of it—so I tend to be quite conversant with everything that's going on, politically and otherwise. C. tends not to be. I've tried to get him to do this, but O. could be run over by a truck and I suspect that C. may not know of it for several days, while *I* would know it the minute he hit the hospital.

It is quite possible that the strain of campaigning produces this mutual dissatisfaction. Or alternatively, this candidate and manager may each be correct in his assessment of the other. The reader may wonder why these two joined forces. But when a candidate is beginning an underdog campaign, or if he does not have much political experience, he may have to settle for any experienced campaign manager, whether or not their views on the running of the race coincide. Similarly, a manager in need of a candidate may find very few people willing to make the race. In short, especially in challengers' campaigns, a great deal of conflict between candidates and managers may be found.

In summary, one's position in the campaign has an impact on his role cognitions. Candidates tend to be more "outside" oriented than managers. Candidates do more talking with voters and believe that they *should* have more contact with voters. They are more personally involved in the success of the campaign, and their goals extend beyond simply winning, to include the benefits of winning a big victory. Candidates are also more attached to tradition than managers are. Perhaps because their feelings and hopes are so tied up in the campaign, candidates tend to prefer tested methods, a definite campaign plan, and clear cues from their environment. Perhaps the candidates can reassure themselves by limiting the innovation in the campaign. If they cannot be sure that they will win, at least they can have the security of using campaign methods that have worked before and the knowledge that their campaign staff has its marching orders.

Managers, in contrast, are less oriented toward voters and more toward organization. They are more innovative and willing to accept change, more pragmatic, and less concerned with the subtleties of winning a bigger victory. Given these findings it is easy to understand why managers might be more favorably impressed than candidates with the New Politics. Because they are more adaptable to new ideas, less tradition-bound and less concerned with face-to-face contact with voters, managers are more willing to try the New Politics style of campaigning.

These differences between candidates and managers suggest that conflict between the two campaign positions is likely. In fact, a great deal of disagreement was detected within individual campaigns. Some of this internal conflict seemed to be clearly and openly expressed; in other cases, the candidates and managers seemed to function as though they had not a difference in the world.

These intra-campaign conflicts might at times interfere with the smooth operation of a campaign. But they are also a sign of political health. Rather than well-oiled fighting machines, instead we see groups of people who can disagree on many things and yet work toward the same goal. The campaign, like the political party organization, can be a more open institution than many have assumed. It has room for dissent. Many of the Wisconsin campaigns *were* run like military units, refusing to brook disagreement from the workers, but in others there was evidence of open dialogue and pragmatic acceptance of different views.

Summary and Conclusions

Each of these five factors—party, type of election, occupation, incumbency, and position in the campaign—has an impact on representational role cognitions. Democrats are more likely than Republicans to seek out voters' opinions on issues. Lawyers and teachers are much more active in this respect than businessmen. Challengers more than incumbents tend to act as instructed delegates. Statewide campaigners and candidates (rather than managers) are more likely to talk with voters and party leaders as well.

There is a common thread in these findings. Within each set of variables, campaigners who express greater uncertainty about the election result are more likely to make an effort to learn the preferences of voters. This uncertainty stimulates campaigners to use any methods possible to improve their chances. Without uncertainty, campaigners become more complacent. They do not feel the need to communicate with the voters directly. If they do not consider talking with voters worthwhile, now they can act on that belief. As Chapter 2 suggested, uncertainty about the election result is in fact a strong force for responsiveness among political leaders. It encourages them to act as delegates rather than trustees.

On the innovation-tradition dimension, Republicans and incumbents are much more likely than Democrats and challengers to avoid change and maintain tradition. Party and incumbency are the strongest influences on this set of role cognitions. Some stereotypes regarding occupational influences are in evidence: teachers are most flexible, businessmen are most traditional. Although occupation overlaps with all of the other independent variables, this finding has a certain ring of intuitive truth to it. Candidates are also less flexible and more traditional than managers. One notable effect of this last finding is that managers are more receptive to new methods of campaigning, such as the New Politics.

With the exception of position in the campaign, this pattern is familiar. Those groups that accept change and innovation more readily are also more likely to try to learn voters' views. These two role dimensions are related. Any campaigner who plans to represent his district's preferences must have some tolerance for change. Constituents' views change over time. There are great differences in public opinion from one area to another. But there is another link between these two role dimensions. The impact of incumbency strongly influences both dimensions. Incumbents were found to prefer traditional methods in their campaigns. The success associated with these methods assures their continued use. And incumbents were less likely to seek out public opinion during the campaign. Dominating these two role dimensions, incumbency is the most powerful factor affecting the Wisconsin campaigners.

The third role dimension relates to the focus of a campaigner's efforts. Respondents tend to orient themselves toward either the voters (and face-to-face methods of campaigning) or toward the campaign organization (and the mass media). Republicans, managers and incumbents are more likely than their opposite numbers to rely on the media. They probably have different reasons for this choice. Republicans and incumbents are slightly better-funded, and more concerned about conserving their time and energy than conserving money. The managers' pragmatism and acceptance of new techniques makes them more interested in the mass media.

Further, managers are more involved in organizational activities, and the problems and tasks of the volunteers, while candidates show greater interest in voters and opponents. This role dimension, in short, does not reflect the same patterns as the other two. Certainty or uncertainty does not dominate. Rather, campaigners specialize in certain areas of responsibility. This role dimension helps to clarify the contrast between candidates and managers. Their division of labor is natural and logical. Their tasks are distinct and separable. This permits differences of opinion without provoking destructive conflict between the two principal characters. Their different perspectives can thus exist within a campaign organization without tearing it apart.

To conclude, campaigners' reactions and perceptions can be classified into at least three role dimensions. They can be seen as delegates or trustees, innovators or traditionalists, and voter-oriented or organization-oriented. In each case the effects of two factors stand out. Incumbency and position in the campaign condition the roles these political leaders play. By tracing these roles, the influences on campaigners' activities and attitudes have become clearer and more patterned. Campaign organizations are made up of several different sets of roles that give structure and direction to the work of winning elections.

6   Conclusion

This book began with a lot of questions. What effects do attitudes, perceptions, and personalities have on campaign decisions? Are candidates any different from managers in their attitudes and behavior? How can we explain differences between the kinds of decisions made in one campaign and those made in another? Now it is time to draw together the answers that have been offered in the preceding chapters and to look at the consequences of these findings.

Readers of newspapers and watchers of television news may be struck by the unique qualities of particular candidates and campaigns, for better or for worse. The sight of high-level Nixon campaign officials discussing their relationship to the Watergate break-in, Ed Muskie tearfully defending his wife on the steps of a New Hampshire newspaper office, George McGovern expressing 1000 percent confidence in a soon-to-be-dumped running mate, Robert Kennedy shot and killed before millions of viewers as he left a victory celebration in California—all these singular events may make an observer tremble at the thought of finding explanations that apply to all campaigns. How is it possible, the observer may ask, to find a generalization that could explain the campaign decision-making of both Bella Abzug and Gerald Ford?

General explanations cannot accomplish miracles, and it is possible that finding many commonalities between Ms. Abzug and Mr. Ford would fall into that category. But many common elements *have* been found. We have seen that a campaign is itself a small socio-political system. Campaigns have members. Campaigns have boundaries from other parts of the political system. Their members operate within certain broad rules: their primary goal is generally conceded to be winning the election, and they must avoid at all costs being caught using unfair campaign practices. Certain traditional activities are expected of them: making at least a few public appearances, proclaiming their belief in the American political system, putting out messages to the voters via at least some of the channels that are considered appropriate for politics, such as mass media, free literature, mass meetings, door-to-door persuasion.

The behavior of campaigners and their organizations, in short, follows some very basic rules. But beyond these broad commonalities, we can also generalize about particular subgroups of campaigners. We can make some predictions about a campaigner's attitudes and behavior once we learn whether he is an incumbent or a challenger, a candidate or a manager, and (to some extent) a Democrat or a Republican. We have seen that incumbents approach politics differently than challengers do, and that candidates tend to perform certain functions that differ from those of managers. These jobs are not interchangeable, at least in the Wisconsin campaigns.

Three types of influences on campaigners help us to understand their attitudes and behavior. First, the campaigner's personality and his psychological makeup lead him to make certain kinds of choices. This study has only begun to chart the effects of personality and psychological stress on campaign decision-making. We have looked at only one personality trait: tolerance-intolerance of ambiguity. It has a forceful influence on the campaigner's willingness to accept changes in campaigns and affects his choice of campaign style. Psychological stress is associated with the amount of effort he puts into his campaign.

The second major influence, position in the campaign, affects a broader range of campaign activities. In fact, candidates and managers differ in nearly every area of decision-making. They differ in their willingness to meet directly with voters, their acceptance of new ideas and new techniques in campaigning, and their attitudes toward the New Politics, party leaders, newspapermen, and campaign volunteers. To generalize about their behavior, we can conclude that candidates are much more likely to be found in voter-contact activities because they see themselves as ambassadors from the organization to the outside. Looking at their attitudes, we can generalize that candidates are more ego-involved in campaigning. Their personality traits are more likely to be reflected in their campaign activities and decisions. They are more likely to respond to goals other than just winning: goals involving their political future, their relationship with the voters, and their own desire to be esteemed by others.

Finally, the campaigner's chances of winning the election strongly affect his attitudes and behavior. We observed this influence by looking at two questions: whether the respondent was certain or uncertain about the election result, and whether he was an incumbent or a challenger. There was a strong association between incumbency and assurance about the election result, between challengers and uncertainty. And there is good reason why this combination of influences should leave its mark on campaign decision-making. Most campaigners say that the chief goal of any campaign should be victory on election night. If victory is the primary reason for the long hours, the frazzled nerves and the money spent, then the campaigner's chances of winning will loom large in his decision-making about the campaign.

We can think of a candidate or manager's chances of winning as the "distance" between himself and election victory—the proximity of victory, as he sees it. Three general predictions can be made. The greater the distance a campaigner sees between himself and election victory, (1) the more effort he is likely to expend in every area of campaigning; (2) the more likely he is to take chances with new methods, new workers, and new appeals; and (3) the more he is stimulated to learn about public opinion on issues. A campaigner whose chances look slim is likely to see these activities as ways to keep himself in the race.

Each of the three major influences on campaign strategy—personality, position in the campaign, and proximity of victory—has consequences for the future of campaigning and for the operation of the democratic process. Now let us explore these consequences in detail.

Personality and Democratic Politics

People who are more tolerant of ambiguity are also more likely to accept changes in campaigns. This relationship is important in the evolution of campaigning. The ability of campaigns to develop and grow depends on the willingness of the participants to make changes and innovations.

If this one personality trait affects campaign decision-making, then other personality traits may also be important. We have a great deal to learn about the kinds of personality traits that influence campaign decisions and the kinds of personalities that are attracted to politics. The interaction between personality and politics is a fascinating area for study. But it is not just a matter of academic interest. As was mentioned in Chapter 1, political leaders strongly influence the shaping of this nation's political life. And some personality traits are probably more compatible with democratic behavior than others are. Although there is no one-to-one relationship through which a personality trait can run a country, a campaigner who lacks democratic traits might be able to do some damage to the operation of a democratic election.

While this is not meant to define a democratic personality, some personality traits that could be considered more compatible with democratic behavior might include a willingness to abide by the rules (of an election), the ability to control one's need for achievement or power so that electoral defeat can be accepted, a tolerance of dissent (whether that dissent comes from outside groups, one's opponent, or co-workers), respect for the rights of others, and of course tolerance of ambiguity. Democratic politics generally contains a lot of ambiguity and a lot of temptation. Public opinion is murky and changeable. Many political events can be interpreted equally well as helping or hurting a candidate. A political system in which decisions are almost always reversible could be a nightmare for someone whose stock of tolerance for ambiguous situations is low.

But what happens if a campaigner for high office does not have these democratic personality traits? Suppose we have a campaign led by people who like things to be clear-cut. They prefer an organization in which everyone knows his place and no one steps out of line. They believe that people will try to avoid work unless they are given orders. In their opinion, people need direction and luckily, people also *like* direction; therefore people must be directed by those who "think right." Further, general discussion about campaign goals is not a good thing. It just produces confusion. In fact, dissent within the public is not a very good thing either, especially when it touches on matters that are important to the national welfare. Rather, people inside and outside the campaign must understand that when the leaders examine all the alternatives and choose a direction, it should be followed promptly. The followers must understand the need for their loyalty. Disloyalty to the leaders is like disloyalty to a higher cause, and it cannot be pardoned.[1]

This picture raises a lot of questions. Will a campaigner like this be tempted to "influence" the election results because he believes that he *must* be elected? Will he follow the same style of leadership if he wins office? Or will he simply scare the voters and lose? In 1964 there was a presidential campaign with relatively little tolerance for ambiguity, and it did in fact lose. The candidate was Barry Goldwater, a man described by Karl Lamb and Paul Smith as reluctant to compromise and determined to run a highly organized campaign. He required loyalty from his staff and dedication to a certain vision of conservatism. The kinds of strong principles and personalities of the campaign's leaders made his race unique in modern politics. It also sounded suspiciously like the organization of a person trying to limit and control ambiguity by creating a tightly organized campaign. But in the process it frightened a lot of voters and failed. One of its central articles of faith, that a hidden majority of conservatives who had never before found a candidate to their liking would emerge to elect a president in 1964, proved to be without foundation.[2]

The kind of campaign run by Goldwater, Lamb and Smith feel, is not very widespread. They see it as an example of a model that they term *comprehensive* : a campaign organization that prefers to gather every relevant bit of information before making decisions. The comprehensive campaign dislikes ambiguity and makes every effort to fence it in with plans, facts, and lines of authority. The planning is done by spreading a wide net for information, categorizing and analyzing it, and coming up with the very best alternative for action. The authority is maintained by a few people at the top giving orders to those below.[3]

The opposition campaign in that election year was very different from Senator Goldwater's. Lyndon Johnson and his campaign tolerated confusion, relied on tradition, welcomed bargaining and compromise. Johnson's long-range vision of American politics, if he had one, was overshadowed by his interest in immediate solutions to immediate problems. An organization chart probably would have meant little to him; he could not have confined himself to one box in it. He rarely delegated authority voluntarily. He enjoyed the process of creating agreement, the contact and the bargaining, and he took part in it all over the campaign.[4]

In both of these campaigns the personalities of the people in charge were able to shape an organization that was either more, or less, in tune with tolerance and informality, and the campaign that disliked ambiguity lost. But this is not always the case. Testimony before the Senate Select Committee on Presidential

Campaign Activities (the so-called Watergate hearings) indicated that some members of the 1972 Nixon campaign operated on principles that were at best on the margin of democracy. Leaders of that campaign described to the Senate committee their concern for loyalty, hierarchy, discipline, and obedience. Some of them believed that dissenting groups were a part of a nationwide conspiracy that was using the opposition campaign to threaten the nation. As a result, perhaps out of an excess of loyalty, some employees of the campaign were driven to commit burglary and espionage in order to learn the opponent's plans. Even beyond loyalty, some campaign staff members believed that the re-election of the president was more important to the country's well-being than was the upholding of an independent judiciary or a nonpartisan Department of Justice.[5]

The Nixon campaign in 1972 looked like a shoe-in from the beginning, and yet some campaign activists resorted to these desperate tactics as though the election were uncertain. Many people have asked why. Perhaps the campaign's advisers were not as confident as people have assumed. There is some evidence that the personalities and experiences of the campaign's top people led them to expect a strong opposition and to respond accordingly. Richard Nixon and his close associates had been through several close elections together and some close defeats. After many battles with the press, they seemed to see themselves surrounded by untiring critics. Since they believed, as many political leaders do, that they knew the best way to guide the nation, they might have felt that the high level of "dangerous criticism" justified their efforts in return, just to give themselves a fair chance. People who believe that they have the truth, and that others are trying to suppress the truth (no matter whether they are liberals or conservatives) may well feel that they must engage in campaigning that stretches the generally accepted limits.

Most campaigns, including the 1970 Wisconsin campaigns described here, seem to be well within ethical and legal limits in spite of popular suspicions to the contrary. But the 1972 election shows that campaigns designed to eliminate uncertainty can sometimes be successful. If these campaign excesses are related to certain kinds of personalities, then we need to take a closer look at the personalities that are attracted to politics and the ways they react to political pressures. There is always the possibility that personality traits incompatible with democracy could affect the behavior of leaders in office.[6]

But simply studying political personalities is not enough. We must also think about safeguards that can prevent antidemocratic personalities from leaving their mark on American politics. Since very few people have seriously contemplated giving personality tests to political candidates as a condition of running, we must rely on voters' ability and willingness to weed out candidates who will not play fair. For many reasons voters may not be adequately prepared to do this. Grammar and high schools tend to stress the dangers of political conflict and partisanship.[7] And Americans have traditionally held an ambivalent view of the politician. While we tend to admire and respect powerful positions, we often assume that anyone holding these positions is corrupt, inefficient, and ambitious enough to be distrusted.[8] The combination of a relatively taboo subject and an ambivalent view of politics does not help voters to judge candidates sensibly. If political education provided students with more realistic expectations about party conflict, then adults might be better able to hold politicians to certain standards of conduct, rather than assuming that those standards are never met.

Tighter limits on campaign spending and campaign contributions could eliminate some temptation. Careful restriction of the government's ability to stifle dissent in the press by political pressure or by the selective renewal of broadcast licenses can help maintain the freedom of the press to point out excesses in campaigning. The use of political debates can also bare candidates' personalities to the public. But ultimately the burden falls on the voters to show that people who cannot accept the rules of the game are simply not effective in winning votes.

In short, the nature of campaigners' personalities can be vitally important. This is not to say that personality traits are the only determinants of a campaigner's actions; they are not. But if campaigns are to supply the kind of leadership that nurtures democracy, then we should know more and teach more about the principles and personalities of the people who are running those campaigns.

Candidates versus Managers

At the beginning of this book campaign manager Lucy Van Pelt expressed her anguish at the behavior of her candidate Linus (he had capped a very successful campaign with a speech about the coming of the Great Pumpkin, which subsequently reduced his margin of victory from an expected 99 percent to 51 percent). Her exasperation has probably been repeated in real campaigns all over the nation. The positions of candidate and manager are specialized but dependent on one another, and their viewpoints are different enough to provoke some conflict.

This finding of differences between candidates and managers is important to an understanding of campaigns. In fact, these differences are perhaps the most important finding of this book. They begin to chart a field that has not received detailed attention before. The differences are significant for two reasons.

First, they tell us that the campaign organization is not composed of generalists but of specialists. The candidate and manager play reciprocal roles. The activities of each position depend on the activities of the other. Campaigns may also contain specialists in other areas, such as fund-raising, publicity-getting, and issue-defining, and these positions may also have distinctive viewpoints. But even if the analysis is restricted to the two leading campaign positions, it becomes apparent that the division of labor within campaigns can help shape campaigners' decisions, just as their personalities and experience affect their decisions.[9] Someone who has become a candidate, no matter what his political orientations are, will probably perform different tasks and look at campaigning from a different point of view than will someone who has become a manager.

Second, these candidate-manager differences show that most campaigners tolerate at least some conflict within their own campaign. Besides accepting disagreement from their opponents, they can also accept at least some disagreement from other members of their own team. This finding conflicts with the traditional view that the candidate's ideas are always carried out by his appendages, the staff. We *can* find campaigns in which the candidate is surrounded by yes-men who will do virtually anything if ordered. But in many of these Wisconsin campaigns, an order by the candidate functioned simply as an invitation to discuss the matter.[10]

Since open discussion of problems is usually regarded as good for a democracy, it is comforting that such discussion takes place *within* campaigns as well as among them. One observer, Harry Eckstein, has written that stable democracies can contain some subsystems that are run in an authoritarian manner, such as the family and the school, so long as the structures that are closest to the government (for example, parties and campaigns) are democratically run. This congruence in authority patterns between the government and adjacent institutions helps to maintain stable democracy.[11] If we accept this view, then the dissent that is tolerated within many campaigns contributes to the democratic character of American politics. It must not be forgotten, however, that some campaigns do *not* permit dissent, and that such a campaign, if it is large enough and determined enough, may be able to threaten a democratic election effectively.

The division of labor between candidates and managers seems to be well-balanced. The candidate concentrates on the voters; the manager tends to the staff. Each can become skilled in a particular area of campaigning. The manager tries to keep things flexible, remains open to new ideas, and the candidate's enthusiasm for tradition provides a certain ballast. How does such a division of labor develop? Do candidates choose people to be their managers who are expert in methods, pragmatic, or innovative? Or do the views and activities of the two groups diverge as a result of their experience in the campaign? There is evidence of both these pathways among the Wisconsin campaigners but most commonly, roles develop as a result of campaign exposure.

One small congressional campaign provides a good example of a candidate and manager who chose one another because of their already-existing skills. The campaign, a personal mission to spread the conservative philosophy in a district long represented by a liberal Democrat, was doomed from the start. The candidate had run before and he did not expect to do any better this time. If he won, he joked like another determined conservative, he'd demand a recount. Not surprisingly, the state party shared his view of his chances and gave him a tiny budget. He could raise little money on his own. He could not afford billboards, radio ads, or any of the other accoutrements of a respectable campaign. All he could manage were a steady stream of tiny newspaper ads, which he used to poke fun at liberals and to boost his own spirits. But in spite of his barely noticeable showing, the candidate enjoyed the campaign greatly. Expressing an unpopular but well thought-out philosophy meant a great deal to him. He thrived on discussions of political theory. Campaign methods and strategy were much less interesting.

This man recruited as his manager an experienced political technician who had divided loyalties. In addition to the philosopher's campaign, he was managing a "live" campaign for a state legislative candidate. The manager saw hope for the state candidate despite the Democratic tone of the district, and as a pragmatic man he had relatively little interest in the losing congressional campaign. In fact, the congressional race caused him some tension because he did not like to lose. His enthusiasm was totally absorbed in making a good fight for the state legislative seat. The candidate for Congress and his manager did not express any animosity toward one another. They needed each other. The candidate was one of the few people willing to make the race that they both agreed should be made, and the manager had campaign expertise. Very early in the campaign they clearly did not share the same goals. And after the race was over they still did not share the same goals. Once the race was lost, the candidate wrote, "This was a token campaign. I would like to have run a fully-staffed and financed campaign instead." The manager's reaction was, "I would have spent even less."

These kinds of problems were common in the case of minority-party challengers. One of the major sources of conflict in the campaigns was the feeling of one campaigner that the other was not putting enough time or talent into the race. The problem was compounded by the pressures of an uphill fight. When things are not going well, people tend to look for scapegoats. After election day there is pressure on a losing candidate to blame his loss on the voters' lack of intelligence or independence. It is not surprising that a campaigner may look for some relief from his personal responsibility *during* the campaign as well. His differences with his campaign co-worker can provide a handy outlet. As election day in Wisconsin drew nearer, it was not uncommon for candidates and managers to privately blame one another for lack of energy, bad judgment, inadequate attention to detail, or simply general ineptness.

In contrast, the campaigns of incumbents tended to be more harmonious, and the candidates and managers tended to develop more specialized positions as time went on. Take, for example, two men who had begun campaigning together over a decade before. They started as underdogs but they were vitally concerned with representing a liberal vision of politics that they both shared. Their first campaign and their first term of office were a baptism of fire. While their dedication to issues remained largely unchanged, their habits of politicking had to change. The demands on the congressman's time grew and he tended to overschedule himself. The manager, now the congressman's administrative assistant, began to insist that all requests for speeches and appearances be channeled through him. The manager was harder to convince of the virtues of a particular speaking engagement, so he was able to reduce the demands on the candidate's energy.

Neither the candidate nor the manager was very fond of campaigning. The candidate regretfully concluded that many issues were "ground up" in a campaign and that campaigning could not be the educational experience he desired. But still his main interest was in the issues that could be raised. He knew the strengths and weaknesses of particular campaign methods, but he was happy to let those details be handled by others. The choice of methods he somewhat distastefully termed "tactics" as opposed to "strategy."

The candidate did not have time to become involved with the campaign organization, so the manager began spending most of his time in the head-quarters working with the staff. The manager's interest in campaigning was still slim, but he developed more and more expertise in organizing those tactics and in developing a strong sense of the direction of public opinion. He was skeptical about really understanding what influenced voters, but he took pride in being able to predict accurately the trend of the election from factors such as the head of the ticket's popularity and the name recognition level of the opponent. He learned skills in areas where the candidate could not become involved. His capabilities, then, developed along the same lines as most managers: running the campaign staff, making decisions about method use, and scheduling the candidate's time.

In most cases campaign leaders begin to specialize in particular tasks because there is a great deal to be done and the range of necessary jobs is very wide. If candidates and managers both spend their days meeting voters, there would be no one to check on the efforts of their staffs. The expectations of outside groups also increase the need for specialization. It is taken for granted that a candidate who wants to be elected should go out and meet groups of voters at least occasionally. The pressures of election uncertainty cause many candidates to spend most of their time meeting voters. If the candidate must devote his time to this duty, then the scheduling, the organizing, and the getting out of mailings or brochures must be left to someone else. Not many candidates rebel against this arrangement. The need of many candidates for widespread approval and esteem requires that they spend a lot of time telling voters about themselves.

No matter how broad their interest in politics may be, persons who become actively involved in campaigns tend to specialize. They specialize because it is an efficient method of handling election tasks and because they are more interested in some aspects of campaigning than others. Managers rarely specialize in winning crowds and candidates seldom specialize in keeping the staff organized. The traditions of campaigning and the expectations of outside groups teach campaigners what roles they must play. The learning of these roles does not always take place during the first campaign, but over time it tends to direct candidates and managers into characteristic patterns of activity.

A Learning Approach to Campaign Strategy

Candidates and managers each learn behavior and attitudes appropriate to their positions. The concept of learning can also help us understand the importance of incumbency and tradition in this study. Learning involves changes in attitudes and behavior. It often refers to a process of adapting to a situation by modifying one's actions or beliefs to become more acceptable or more useful in that situation.[12] Social psychologists tell us about several methods of learning. In some cases we learn to choose a particular behavior out of a wide range of possible behaviors because one activity is reinforced—rewarded or encouraged. The example of pigeons learning to ring bells when they are rewarded with food for doing so comes readily to mind. People too tend to repeat behaviors that bring desired responses and to drop behaviors that are not reinforced.

But this model of conditioning takes time. A campaigner generally does not have the time to run through all possible campaign behaviors to see which ones will be rewarded. He must make choices quickly. And he can use a shortcut to learn what behaviors are likely to be reinforced. Looking around him, he may see one or more successful politicians who are comparable to him in some ways. Perhaps an incumbent congressman espouses the same positions on issues as he does. Or another incumbent won his first race in the same kind of district or against similar opposition. The new candidate or manager can then use this successful campaigner as a model, adopting many of the same methods, issues, organization, or general style. Imitation of a successful model speeds the campaigner along the road to shaping his campaign. From there he is likely to continue behaviors that are reinforced and to change those that are not. As one new candidate stated:

Especially when you're carrying on your first political campaign you have to rely largely on what others tell you. And it may be that after the campaign is over and we start to evaluate it, we may discover things that very well might have been eliminated, and other things that should have been done.

There are several kinds of possible reinforcement. Approval from co-workers or party leaders, good words in the press, personal gratification from doing what is right, can all reinforce certain behaviors or beliefs. The most dramatic form of reinforcement comes from the voters: winning a majority of votes on election day, or winning by a larger-than-expected margin. For many campaigners, activities reinforced by one of these sources tend to be rewarded by other sources as well. Co-workers and party leaders appreciate a winning campaign and are likely to give positive signs to a candidate and manager to whom the voters are also giving positive signs. But this does not always have to be the case. For example, a candidate who is running mainly to represent a particular point of view, such as the philosopher of the last section, may find himself reinforced by members of the press and certain active volunteers who share his views even while he is being punished by the voters. If the campaigner values the opinions of others who have rewarded him more than the opinions of "uninformed voters," if the benefits that election victory brings him are secondary to the benefits of running an issue campaign, then the candidate may continue to behave the same way in his next campaign even though his behavior may appear defeatist or illogical to an outsider.

But for most campaigners the fruits of victory are more important than the approval of newspapermen or volunteers. Most candidates and managers campaign to win office, not to discuss issues with the public or meet interesting people at the headquarters. Therefore we can look at campaigns as a learning process in which new participants often choose a model because they do not have the time or the desire for trial-and-error approaches, and in which election victory is the major agent of reinforcement, causing campaigners to repeat methods and strategies that are reinforced and to drop others.

Let us look at examples of the learning process that follows the election result. The Wisconsin campaigners were contacted after the election and asked whether they could think of any changes they would like to have made in the 1970 campaign. Here are some of their own evaluations of their campaigns:

Regarding organization—
"I needed more staff, especially (1) press and public relations person, (2) office manager and secretary, (3) finance chairman."
"Needed more volunteers."
"Would have had more *paid* help. Had difficult time getting volunteers (who would work)."
"I should have spent more time on careful selection of campaign coordinators in each county and gotten to know them more, personally."

Regarding methods—
"I wouldn't have used cartops or yard signs [again]. Too expensive."
"Earlier TV production."
"Distribution of materials should have been done earlier."
"More appearances of candidate before nonpartisan groups."
"Get the candidate to campaign more, *much* more. That would facilitate the organizing activities."
"[Would have] talked to more groups; made more group appeals. Tried to make individual appeals—impossible in large district."

Regarding issues—
"I would not have relied as much on polls as [on] innate sense, and would have changed issue emphasis [to] economy rather than law and order."

"More aggressive in attacking our opposition's voting record."

"Better reaction to negative or critical advertising and comments by the opposition against the record of the incumbent administration."

Perhaps the most common evaluation was expressed by one campaigner:

"Organization was a problem which we hope to solve by getting an early start next time."

As many responses indicate, these evaluations of the current campaign are not just expressions of wistful regret. They are also the beginnings of plans for the future. Most of the comments came from people who had lost the election. They came into the campaign with a set of ideas, perhaps drawn from previous campaigns or those of other successful politicians, or perhaps drawn from their own mental image of the way a campaign should operate. At the end of the campaign they were judged. If they lost, and if they maintain any hope of future political success, then they must assess their campaign decisions and find the mistakes. However, the election result—the major agent of reward or punishment—is a powerful teacher but not a very informative one. It rewards campaigns that include many dozens of different behaviors and punishes others that contain some of the same behaviors. The voting returns do not state clearly which of the campaign's behaviors are being rewarded or which are being condemned. They simply say "pass" or "fail." The campaigner's learning process takes place in an atmosphere of uncertainty. He does not know exactly what he did right and what he did wrong.

If he won, it may not matter that he lacks this information. But if he lost, the problem is especially difficult. As one unhappy defeated manager noted:

Before [the election] you have a good idea, but after it's over you have grave doubts. When you win, everything you did was right. And if you lose, everything you did was all wrong. So I do have many doubts—but in losing, you wonder what the hell you *could* have done that *would* have made any difference.

The losing campaigner may be alerted to particular trouble spots. For example, if he did well in county A and poorly in county B, he will know where to concentrate the changes in approach when he runs again. If he hears several people saying that his television ads were an unmitigated disaster, he will probably change them rather than touching his radio ads, which were praised highly. A losing campaigner may be able to localize the trouble but he cannot be sure that even if he made changes in all the trouble spots, those changes would turn the tide. He may decide what he *should not* have done, but it is harder to know what *should* have been done to assure victory.

Winning campaigners may have a more pleasant evaluation process and they may feel more assured about their progress during the campaign, but after election day they too have very little information on which to base refinements or changes. Because they cannot be certain what aspects of their campaign won the election for them, they are very likely to repeat everything in their next campaign. Politicians tend to express satisfaction, even identification, with the techniques they used in winning campaigns, and future campaigns will probably be a variation on the same theme. The manager of a winning candidate, explaining why he would not have made any changes in the 1970 campaign, pointed out, "we can't beat success."

Many students of politics have questioned whether a body of knowledge exists that would enable campaigners to anticipate accurately and direct successfully the responses of the voters.[13] One writer reports that most campaign specialists have enough doubts about their own theories of managing campaigns to continue working by trial and error.[14] In this uncertain learning process a successful campaigner might well be reluctant to change anything about a winning campaign, including the covers of his matchbooks. So the patterns of winning campaigns can easily become stabilized.

In short, the election results and the accompanying uncertainty affect campaigners' choices in *subsequent* elections. We might also expect that a campaigner's feelings about how well he is doing in a particular race—the perceived proximity of victory—will affect his behavior and decisions *during* that campaign too. It was suggested that a campaigner becomes aware of the likely election result well before election day, so the expected voting returns can condition his behavior during the campaign. For instance, campaigners who will later lose the election say that they feel more stress during the race. We have also seen that incumbents and challengers, who differ very clearly in whether they expect to win, have quite different attitudes and activities during the campaign.

The coming election verdict can affect campaigners both directly and indirectly. In a direct way, most candidates and managers are interested in learning how the voters are reacting to their campaign. If some feedback—polls, newspaper articles, or simply scuttlebut—indicates that some part of the campaign is failing, most campaigners are stimulated to work on that aspect. Since their goal, usually, is election victory, information about their success in reaching that goal affects their thinking about the campaign.

But the progress of the campaign affects people in an indirect way too. People's responses to a campaign are conditioned in part by its winning or losing atmosphere. Party activists, for example, often monitor local campaigns to determine the candidates' likelihood of success. They can put pressure on a likely loser by limiting the input of party funds in order to concentrate the money in campaigns more likely to win. Volunteers are less likely to flock to a losing campaign. Even the manager of a likely loser may write off the campaign. A great deal of pressure can build around a campaigner headed for defeat. An underdog campaigner, by the force of his own personality and aspirations, may maintain confidence in spite of the odds and therefore overcome some of this stress. But generally the expected outcome of a campaign is reflected in the reactions of all those who deal with it. During the campaign as well as afterwards, it affects the choices of the participants.

This learning approach to campaign decision-making can be seen in many other campaigns, both recent and long-past. The diffusion of a new idea or model can often be traced to many different areas in a relatively short period of time. For example, several years ago a young Republican congressional challenger in Michigan caught his district's attention by going into crowds with his sport jacket slung loosely over his shoulder, looking earnest, relaxed and approachable. His billboards reflected this pose. After the challenger won and this innovation was reported, this style (particularly the coat slung over the shoulder, the tie hanging determinedly askew) was copied by new campaigners all over the country, sometimes to their regret. A Wisconsin campaigner described his opponent's use of this style, pointing out with amusement that while it obviously worked in suburban Michigan, it did not go over well when transplanted into a university town's cocktail parties.

Similarly, when 1970 senatorial candidate Lawton Chiles (now D.–Fla.) won a campaign that included a long walk from one end of the state to the other, several other senatorial and gubernatorial candidates followed suit. The 1972 election was replete with long marches and worn out hiking boots. One potential candidate went so far as to announce that he would *swim* from one end of his state to the other. (Fortunately he too lived in Florida.) This diffusion of successful innovations is hastened by the tendency of radio and television to pick up an unusual story. But it also reflects the great interest of new campaigners, and those who face unexpected opposition, in finding techniques that show some evidence of success.

There is evidence that other campaign methods have come into widespread use as a result of the victory of one or more successful innovators. Presidential candidates early in the last century traditionally conducted inactive front porch campaigns, but over a relatively long period, the success of active presidential campaigners such as William McKinley, Theodore Roosevelt and Franklin Roosevelt convinced later presidential hopefuls that an active campaign was a must. Television as a campaign technique was first used extensively by the 1952 Eisenhower presidential campaign.[15] The short spot advertisements developed for Eisenhower, emphasizing his personal qualities and strength, were a major part of his very successful introduction to politics. Since that time no major presidential candidate has dared to ignore the use of that medium.

Tracing the spread of innovations is an intriguing job,[16] and it can be done currently by following the spread of New Politics techniques such as sophisticated polling, the use of television, and highly organized managerial styles. For example, the use of computers to direct mass mailings on particular issues to individuals who would be interested in those issues--sending material on defense policy to persons on computerized lists of subscribers to foreign policy journals or military-oriented magazines, for example—seems likely to move into more high-budget campaigns in the near future.

In short, we see both traditionalism and the spread of innovations in campaigning. Both can be explained by looking at campaigns as a learning process. The diffusion of new campaign methods is a part of the process by which new and underdog campaigners seek successful models of campaigns on which to pattern their own efforts. Starting from the premise that most campaigners are out to win, and that there are no sure ways of securing a victory, campaigners must look for cues to determine what will have a high probability of success. Inexperienced campaigners will often take their cues from other people—advice from those with more experience, or perhaps media reports of other successful campaigns. When a candidate successfully uses a new technique and his activities are reported in the media, his experience may become part of a new campaigner's learning process. If the new technique is used in a winning campaign, and if the district or the race is comparable, the new campaigner may decide to take the plunge and adopt the innovation. New campaigners may also adopt the ideas of established political experts, advertising agencies, or even an ideal vision of a campaign that they themselves have developed. Incumbents are more likely to rely on their own models, their own tested practices, rather than risking a disruption of their pattern of success by trying new approaches.

We return to this concept: behaviors that work will be retained, and behaviors that fail will probably be dropped. Incumbents may not know the exact reasons for their victories, but they do know that *some* of their methods must have gone over well, and so most of their methods will probably be continued. Challengers may either use trial-and-error methods of improving on their past campaigns, or they may imitate models, either relatively innovative or quite traditional. Their choice probably has a lot to do with their attitudes and personalities, their willingness to accept the kind of uncertainty associated with trying new methods, and their general tendency to take risks or go with a sure thing.

Learning is a form of adaptation. Learning to be a campaigner likewise involves adaptation. Candidates and managers tend to respond to those cues in their environment that tell them about possible victory or defeat. Their likelihood of success conditions their activities. Individual campaigners also respond to the structure of the campaign. Their position as a candidate or a manager influences their views and behavior. The proximity of victory and position in the campaign are among the strongest explanatory factors in campaign decision-making.

But the campaign itself adapts too. It adapts not only to its environment but to the experience, attitudes and personality traits of the candidates and managers. On occasion a campaigner who should win easily, and who plays his position well, has "snatched defeat from the jaws of victory." So the makeup of the individual campaigner can affect the kind of learning process he experiences, and the way he reacts to the events of the campaign. Personality and attitudes, expressed within the structured features of campaigns, do have an impact on campaign decision-making. And that impact can cast its shadow over the democratic nature of American politics.

Appendix

Appendix

Methodology

As with the running of a campaign, no research project could go forward
without the preparation that takes place behind the scenes. Yet the methods of
building a study, gathering and analyzing data are not often discussed fully. In
the belief that such a discussion enables other researchers to better judge the
data presented, and also gives new researchers some solutions to common
problems, this appendix will describe in detail the survey design and analysis
used in this study.

Writing the Interview Schedule

Formulating questions for the interview may be the most important step in
survey research. The most sophisticated data analysis techniques cannot make up
for a set of badly formulated or uninteresting survey items. Two vital tests of
interview questions are whether they are adequate in operationalizing the main
concepts of the study, and whether they are written so that the responses can be
compared with those of other studies in the same field. A survey of the literature
can be very helpful for ensuring that the present research *is* comparable with
other studies, to increase our scientific understanding of campaigning.

This study began with a literature search in the general fields of campaigns,
party organization, and organizational psychology. Hypotheses about campaigning that had been previously tested were listed and compared, with several ideas
sifted out for replication. Other studies also suggested variables for inclusion in
this questionnaire.[1] The main reason for the study—to determine the effects of
personality and attitude variables on campaigners' behavior and concerns—led to
the choice of additional variables to be tested.

Next, specific questions had to be devised for measuring personality and
attitude variables. An excellent compilation of attitude testing instruments by
staff members of the University of Michigan's Survey Research Center was used
to choose a written personality test to be administered after the interview.[2]
Stanley Budner's test of tolerance-intolerance of ambiguity fit well into the
research design. It measures reactions to a condition—ambiguity—that seems
ever-present in political campaigns. It adds another dimension to understanding
the campaigners' flexibility and innovation in decision-making as well.

Budner's test is a paper-and-pencil questionnaire that can be quickly self-
administered, so it did not add much length to the interview. The test also has
the advantages of a generally-accepted interpretation, ease of coding, and lack of
significant bias. Budner's scale consists of sixteen items, with eight worded

positively and eight worded negatively. He selected items that could each represent one of the three components that he found in this personality trait: insolubility, complexity and novelty.

Because of the severe time constraints involved in interviewing campaigners, the sixteen-item scale was reduced to eight items. The new scale was drawn to contain the same proportions of positively and negatively worded items and of the trait's three components, as in the original scale. Several criteria were used to shorten the scale to eight items. First, the original scale was designed for a cross-section of citizens while the shorter scale would be administered to political leaders. Because of the difference between these groups, several of the original items no longer seemed appropriate and therefore were eliminated. For example, Budner's item "I would like to live in a foreign country for a while" (representing novelty) might strike a congressman much differently from an average worker, since most congressmen are likely to have had the opportunity to travel in other nations.

The wording of other items seemed to make their purpose obvious to a campaigner. For example, the statement "The sooner we all acquire similar values and ideals the better" might warn a campaigner, even more than an average citizen, that the interviewer is concerned about individual freedom to dissent. Whether or not this is actually the case, the respondent's answers may be altered because he suspects this purpose. The sensitivity of most politicians to questions that could be used against them made these items dispensable.

Using a scale that has already been tested provides the researcher with a time-saving measure of a variable, and a baseline for interpreting his own data. However, any such scale must be carefully examined to see whether it applies to different types of respondents, and adapted if necessary. (The eight-item questionnaire is reproduced at the end of this appendix.)

Budner reports that reliability in a test-re-test study of fifteen graduate students over a two to four week period was .85. Other tests of reliability showed varying degrees of success. He found no significant correlations with a measure of acquiescence response set (the tendency of some respondents to want to agree with the interviewer) or with the Edwards Scale of Social Desirability.[3]

The concept of tolerance-intolerance of ambiguity is defined by Budner as "the tendency to perceive (i.e. interpret) ambiguous situations as sources of threat."[4] It is closely allied with a syndrome of variables that are usually termed "authoritarianism." The relationship is described by Robinson and Shaver:

...the ambiguity scale [of Budner] was found to correlate with conventionality, belief in divine power, attendance at religious services, dogmatism about one's religious beliefs, and favorable attitudes toward censorship. The scale also correlated moderately with F (a balanced version constructed by Christie, Havel, and Seidenberg, 1958). ... Its moderate correlation with the Christie F scale suggests trait overlap, but not complete congruence. Intolerance of ambiguity is most likely just one of several characteristics that contribute to high F scores.[5]

Items in Budner's test were each followed by a seven-point Likert-type scale ranging from "strongly agree" to "strongly disagree." For positively-worded items, strong agreement was scored 7 and strong disagreement 1. For negatively-worded items the scoring was reversed. An individual's total score was computed by summing his scores on all items. In Budner's scoring, the range of respondents' scores could extend from 16 to 112, with lower scores indicating greater tolerance.

Budner reports that he administered his test to several groups of students, ranging from a New York high school English class to medical students in Eastern and Midwestern schools. The mean scores of these classes of students ranged from 43.3 (at a private New York women's college) to 53.0 (at an evening psychology class in a New York college).[6] If the Wisconsin campaigners' scores are computed using Budner's scoring procedure, their mean score is 51.4. The scores of Wisconsin respondents are similar to those of Budner's samples of students. This probably indicates that the Wisconsin campaigners are somewhat more tolerant of ambiguity than the general public, since young people in colleges would be expected to tolerate more ambiguity than the average voter would.

The adapted eight-item scale also used the Likert-type format and Budner's scoring procedure for individual items. But a subject's total score was computed slightly differently. Each respondent's sum of scores on the negatively-worded items was subtracted from his sum of scores on the positively-worded items. The resulting number was his total score. The maximum possible range of scores became −24 to +24. As with Budner's scale, lower (or more negative) scores indicate greater tolerance. The purpose of this change was to move the possible range of scores so that zero represented the mean possible score.

Other kinds of instruments could have been used to test tolerance-intolerance of ambiguity. For example, behavioral tests of this concept have been developed. Two authors used the autokinetic effect (a perceptual illusion in which a stationary point of light appears to be moving) to learn the amount of time it takes for subjects to reach closure in estimating the amount of movement of the light.[7] Administering this kind of test to politicians would provide interesting data. But an attitudinal measure was chosen because this study is primarily concerned with the campaigners' attitudes, and because it would be inconvenient, to say the least, to conduct this kind of test in the middle of a campaign.

Measures of other attitudes were developed and then revised many times with the help of colleagues and political activists. Revisions were done to make the items more concise, more understandable, and more explicit. It was also necessary to reduce the length of the interview schedule as much as possible, and to put the questions in logical order, while sandwiching sensitive questions between less sensitive ones.

The majority of questions in the final interview schedule follow a structured format. For example, in asking a campaigner what kinds of voters a campaign should concentrate on, two alternatives were contained within the narrative of the question: the uncommitted voters or the candidate's likely supporters. If the respondent would not make a choice between these two groups, a standardized probe was used, such as "which group would you emphasize?" The option remained, of course, for the respondent to stay with "neither" or "both." A few questions were relatively structured but open-ended, in that they did not indicate any alternative answers to the respondent. The question "Is there anything you especially dislike about campaigning?" is an example. With these open-ended questions the interviewer would probe ("You are saying, then, that . . . ") only to clarify the remarks the campaigner made, rather than to fit his responses into a particular category.

The structured format assures that each campaigner receives the same question wording in the same order as every other respondent does. Confidence in the comparability of the interviews is increased by this format. In addition, the probes and the complete recording of each answer, even when the respondent digressed, increase the fullness of the information gained about the campaigners, and tell a lot about their frames of reference in dealing with the problems posed by the interviewer.

Pre-Testing

Pre-tests enable the researcher to learn whether his questions are really getting at the dimensions he wants to test. Without these practice runs, he could not be sure that his questions are phrased to keep the respondent's interest without biasing his answers, alienating the respondent or causing him alarm about the interviewer's motives. And the interviewer could not otherwise know how long the answers to particular questions are likely to be. If a particular question elicits long dissertations, then the interviewer is unlikely to have the time to get several other (and possibly more important) questions answered before his subject is anxious to get back to the campaign.

Since all candidates and managers for Congress and statewide office in Wisconsin would be interviewed in the main study, the pre-tests had to be conducted at a different level of government. Campaigners for the Wisconsin State Assembly who were involved in close primary fights seemed the most comparable. The closeness of the primary, it was hoped, would produce concern about the campaign as strong as that of campaigners for higher office.[8] To compensate for the short time available for pre-testing, campaigners who differed in age, ideology, party, and chance of winning were selected, so that the pre-test respondents could represent the characteristics of a larger group of campaigners.[9]

After the pre-tests had been analyzed, several questions in the interview schedule were clarified, some changes were made in question order, and several items were omitted because they tended to stimulate campaign-type oratory about the upholding of democratic norms. The pre-tests also provided an opportunity to test campaigners' reactions to the use of a tape recorder. I learned, in yet another demonstration of the importance of little things, that respondents were very conscious of the tape recorder when it was placed in front of them, and often became quite grave and cautious in choosing their words. But they were much less likely to pay attention to the recorder if it were placed several feet to their side. This method seemed to neutralize the inhibiting effect of the tape recorder.

Making Interview Appointments

About two weeks before an intended interview, the prospective interviewee was sent a letter describing the research project, stating that the interview would be kept strictly confidential, and affirming that the interviewer was nonpartisan (at least for the purposes of this research). These reassurances were essential. Many campaigners were naturally suspicious of divulging their campaign plans to an outsider during the height of their effort to win. In some cases, candidates called the Department of Political Science at the University of Wisconsin to confirm that the interviewer was associated with that department, and not using academic credentials to spy for their opposition. (Unfortunately, one such candidate was put in touch with a department professor who had the same name as a worker in his opponent's office; this did nothing to allay his fears.) To further gain the confidence of campaigners, the initial letter emphasized that the research had been discussed with the organizational leadership of both state parties, and that they had agreed to serve as references for any campaigners who wanted further information before agreeing to an interview.

A week after this letter was mailed, I called the campaigner's office, introduced myself and the research project again, and requested an appointment. In two cases where the introductory letter had not arrived before I called, the respondents were much more reluctant to grant an interview. It seems important, then, to establish some credible explanation of the study before an interview is actually asked.

Campaigners usually protested that their schedules were full and that it would be virtually impossible to spare any time for an interview. Yet interviews generally were scheduled promptly. It seemed that these harried reactions were a part of the litany of the campaign, rather than an indication of reluctance to be interviewed.

However, before the interview can be arranged, the interviewee must be located. This is quite a difficult task. The researcher learns that whether he calls the campaigner's office, his headquarters, his associates or his home, the campaigner has either just left or is about to come. If he is about to come and the interviewer calls back later, he has just left. A great deal of stamina is required at this stage of the research. Further, a warning is in order: it is futile to leave a message for the subject at his campaign headquarters or political office. The chances that he will receive it are very slim.

Most respondents were reached after three or four calls, but more than a dozen tries were necessary in some cases. One campaign manager agreed to be interviewed after the researcher's fourth call because, he said, a person who will not call back at least three times cannot be sincerely interested enough to deserve a meeting.

Appointments with congressmen pose a special problem. Congressional staffs are often overprotective of the congressman's time. Asking his office receptionist for an appointment is definitely not a productive strategy. The easiest cases to handle were those in which the congressman's administrative assistant had answered the initial letter. When calling the office I was then able to get in touch with that assistant, and appointments were usually made quickly. Without this advantage, it was helpful to point out that I was from the congressman's home state. It should be noted here that if Congress is on a normal schedule, interviewers should not expect more than a half-hour meeting, except with administrative aides or unusually talkative congressmen.

After an appointment was made, if time permitted, a letter confirming the time, place, and date of the interview was mailed. This helped ensure that the interview had found its way into someone's schedule book. Only four respondents did not appear at the scheduled time.

Interviewing

Interviews took place between August 30, 1970, and election day. Between August 30 and the September primary, candidates without primary opposition were interviewed. This extra week was useful since the campaign provided only eight weeks for interviewing 61 persons.

Most of the congressmen were interviewed in Washington. The others were contacted in their home district. With the exception of one mail and two telephone interviews, all were conducted in person. While personal interviews provide a great deal of information, including the visual cues that help an interviewer evaluate the responses, a telephone or mail contact can still provide the necessary answers to the interview questions.

Interview conditions were generally good. Most of the respondents were interviewed in their campaign or business offices, and the atmosphere was usually quiet. Remaining meetings took place in restaurants, respondents' homes, a motel lobby, and, during part of one interview, on a long sprint between the Rayburn House Office Building and the Capitol.

The main problem in interviewing was lack of time. Campaigners are always running behind schedule. It is helpful to pinpoint the essential questions so that these can be asked early if time is short. Sessions ranged in length from 20 minutes to two and a half hours, averaging 45 minutes to an hour.

Recording the Interview

Many interviewers avoid tape recorders because they feel the respondents will be inhibited. On the other hand, note-taking limits the amount of material that the interviewer can retrieve. In this study a recorder was used in 41 interviews and notes were taken in 16 others. The majority of those 16 interviews did not have the physical facilities for the recorder; either the location lacked electrical outlets or the background noise was too high. Only three respondents requested that the recorder not be used. I found no difference in the length or frankness of responses between the tape-recorded interviews and the others. Perhaps this was because the recorder was small and had a built-in microphone, so that it could be placed outside of the respondent's field of vision. Since campaigners generally seemed aware of the recorder during the first few minutes of the session and sometimes answered cautiously during that time, I asked factual, less sensitive questions at the beginning. As the interview progressed, very few respondents seemed aware that they were being recorded.

The recorder is especially valuable because it provides a complete transcript of the interview. This eliminates the mistakes that can occur when transcribing notes. The recording reminds the interviewer of occasions when he has asked a question differently from the standard form, so that he can interpret the response accordingly. And it indicates, for example, when a respondent has paused an unusually long time before answering, indicating the question might be a sensitive one. Finally, when the interviewer is freed from note-taking, he is able to observe the facial expressions and reactions of the respondents. These cues can tell a lot about the respondent's feelings and can indicate, at times, whether he is answering honestly and with conviction.

The Interviewer Effect

The relationship between interviewer and respondent is a delicate one. The ideal interviewer should gain his subject's trust, encourage full and open answers (but not too full, or there might not be time for later questions), and avoid at all costs slanting the questions or indicating what the answers ought to be. In other words, the interviewer must provide encouragement for his subject's answers, but only within certain limits; he must guide the conversation, but only up to a certain point.

In practice, then, the interviewer's role raises some difficult questions. Should an interviewer ever inject himself into the conversation or should he record answers without comment? Should he indicate approval of what the respondent is saying in order to encourage him, or does that approval slant the answers he will get?

It is probably impossible to be "neutral" in an interview. Even a tape recorder probably brings some responses from the campaigner. And as Lewis Anthony Dexter points out, the interviewer will be perceived as occupying *some* role, no matter how neutral he tries to be.[10] Clearly the interviewer should not enter into conversation to the extent that he is concentrating on expressing his own viewpoints. The purpose of his visit is to learn what the *campaigner* thinks, but this researcher found that several respondents were uncomfortable when the interviewer did not react to their answers. Several asked, "What do *you* think?" These respondents can be reassured if the interviewer expresses agreement or makes an amplifying remark related to the topic under discussion.

It is helpful to use the respondent's own terms when talking with him. Dexter suggests, "the real point is not to establish neutrality for its own sake, but to create a situation in which the informant will tell what is needed."[11] This does not imply that the interviewer must sacrifice his integrity and agree with ideas he finds objectionable. It does mean that a politician in the midst of battle is a very committed person, and an interviewer who shows that he understands those concerns is more likely to win the respondent's confidence. According to Dexter, talking the respondent's language "tells him that the interviewer shares his perspective on whatever he is going to describe; and for all except a very few informants, that is neutrality."[12]

Non-Responses

The response rate was 93 percent. Four of the 61 campaigners refused to be interviewed. Among these were three Democrats and one Republican; one congressional contender and three statewide campaigners; two incumbents and two challengers. Two of the four conducted campaigns that were barely noticeable to the public. In all the characteristics of these non-respondents do not seem to bias the results substantially.

Post-Election Information

A week after the election a one-page questionnaire was sent to all respondents to learn their views about the campaign in retrospect. Letters accompanying these structured questionnaires were as individual as possible, thanking the respondents for the interview and congratulating them on their election or on the conduct of their campaign. (The post-election questionnaire is included at the end of this appendix.) A second wave of questionnaires was mailed on December 2, 1970, after 40 responses had been received. Thirteen more were returned, totalling 53 responses, or 93 percent of those interviewed. A 54th questionnaire arrived the following August, somewhat too late to be tabulated. The four post-election non-respondents included three Republicans and one Democrat, three managers and one candidate, two winners and two losers. All four were involved in congressional races.

Surprisingly, the losing campaigners were the first to return questionnaires. It was expected that they would be less willing to talk about the campaign. But the losers were probably experiencing a let-down due to the sudden disappearance of reporters and supporters. This seemed to make them more receptive to anyone still expressing interest in their efforts.

Two of the returned questionnaires were blank: the subjects, two congressmen whose usually comfortable margins of victory had been drastically pared in the 1970 election, refused to answer the questions. A third congressman whose margin of victory had also been reduced, although not as markedly, did not return a questionnaire. Other data, not presented here, show clearly that the size of a campaigner's victory is meaningful to him, and that a bare majority is generally not satisfactory to an incumbent accustomed to big victories.[13] The evident sensitivity of these three congressmen on the subject of their election lends some support to that finding.

Coding

After the tapes of interviews were transcribed, answers to the closed-ended questions were coded in the categories set forth in the questions. Open-ended questions were analyzed and the answers compressed into as few categories as were consistent with the range of responses. At times responses fell on more than one dimension, and the question was therefore divided into several variables. The first coding was completed in mid-December. Transcripts were coded again in January, 1971, both to estimate intra-coder reliability and to do any necessary recoding. The test-re-test reliability was 91 percent. This underestimates actual reliability, since the recoding accounted for part of the error. Another coder then did a one-sixth sample of the transcripts. Inter-coder reliability was 95 percent.

Analyzing the Data

After gathering data, the researcher must specify the limitations of those data. In this study, data were nominal and ordinal. The population was relatively small. This made the use of controls difficult, since some cells might then contain too few cases to analyze. In some cases controls were run anyway, when necessary, but such results are not definitive. In many cases in this study, however, it was found that the independent variables (such as incumbency, attitudes toward change, etc.) had an additive effect. Rather than controlling for one independent variable because it produces a spurious relationship, hiding the effects of another independent variable, there were indications of interaction among independent variables. As Herbert Hyman points out:

> ... the concept of spuriousness cannot *logically* be intended to apply to antecedent conditions which are associated with the particular independent variable as part of a developmental sequence. Implicitly, the notion of an uncontrolled factor which was operating so as to produce a spurious finding involves the image of something *extrinsic* to the ... apparent cause. Developmental sequences, by contrast, involve the image of a series of entities which are *intrinsically* united or substitutes for one another. All of them constitute a unity and merely involve different ways of starting the same variable as it changes over time. ... Consequently, to institute procedures of control is to remove so-to-speak some of the very cause that one wishes to study.[14]

As an example of a developmental sequence, Hyman cites a psychological explanatory factor (an attitude) and a sociological explanatory factor (objective status). Many such sequences occurred in this study. For example, there was considerable interaction between the status of incumbency and the attitude of assurance about the election result. Although controls for incumbency were used when examining the relationship between assurance-uncertainty and decisions made in the campaign (see Chapter 2), neither incumbency nor assurance is extrinsic to the causal relationship, and there is evident interaction between the two.

Secondly, in analyzing data the researcher must determine what he expects the analysis to achieve. The aim of this study was to specify the nature and strength of relationships, Goodman and Kruskal's gamma was chosen.[15] Gamma, existence of a relationship, its direction, and its power. To test the direction and strength of relationships, Goodman and Kruskal's gamma as chosen.[15] Gamma, as interpreted by Herbert Costner, is a measure of association which estimates the proportional reduction in error when the estimation of the order of cases (or category, for nominal variables) for a single variable is changed to estimating the order of cases of a dependent variable from an independent variable, as specified in the rules of the statistic.[16] Gamma often produces higher absolute values than does Kendall's tau, which can rarely reach its maximum of 1.0, or Somers' d_{yx}. However, it is widely used by social scientists, appropriate for handling ordinal data, meaningful in Costner's terms, comparable among tables with different numbers of cells, and easy to interpret.

A level of significance must also be specified—a level beyond which a relationship among variables will be termed "significant." Different researchers have used different standards. In this study the level of significance was set at .20. Below this level no relationship is deemed to exist. A gamma of .20 to .39 is considered a "moderate" relationship, and a gamma of .40 or greater is termed a "strong" relationship.[17] In the early stages of understanding a field it is important to generate hypotheses for future testing. It seems preferable, then, to err on the side of accepting false hypotheses by setting the level of significance at .20, rather than to err by rejecting true hypotheses.

The use of chi-square to test the existence of relationships was originally planned. Chi-square is normally applied to samples rather than populations. But it can be argued that the responses of a population are actually a sample of the universe of responses of other candidates for office. Therefore, chi-square can be conceptualized to estimate the extent to which the smaller population resembles the responses of the hypothetical universe of campaigners and to indicate the likelihood that any given results might have been due to error in measurement or other chance error. When an interview consists of attitude questions rather than harder data, such an estimation would be useful. Formulas are available for adapting chi-square to studies containing small numbers of cases.[18] And chi-square has the advantage of being widely understood. This permits a wide range of readers to judge the conclusions and compare the results with other studies.

However, for several reasons the use of chi-square was eliminated. The use of significance tests has long been the subject of argument. Heinz Eulau notes that "statistical tests of significance are intended to measure whether differences observed between two or more groups have been produced by random error of *sampling*" (italics added).[19] He notes, further, that in open-ended questions, often several respondents in a population cannot be coded and are therefore classified as non-responses. But those who *were* coded are not necessarily a random sample of all the respondents interviewed in that population. Finally, he points out, when a study is exploratory and hypotheses are being proposed after the data are collected as well as before, the process becomes circular: hypotheses are formed on the basis of the data and the same data are used to test them. Using significance tests can give a false impression of validity. For these reasons chi-square was not used.

Preliminary data analysis was conducted using a counter-sorter. This pre-analysis was helpful in pointing out certain patterns that the data analysis should take into account. For example, differences between candidates and managers, which had been suspected during interviews, were confirmed in this counter-sorter analysis. These differences were so prominent that the decision was made to analyze the two groups of campaigners separately.

Data analysis was accomplished using the XTAB program of the Data and Computation Center of the University of Wisconsin, on a Univac 1108 computer. Data were analyzed using cross-tabulations. When a campaigner did not answer a question, or when a question was not applicable to a respondent, he or she was not included in the cross-tabulation. Therefore, the number of cases in some tables is smaller than the total population of 57 campaigners.

Respondents and Interview Procedures

Campaigners for Congress

All of Wisconsin's ten congressional seats were contested in 1970. Candidates and managers in congressional races can be described as follows:

	Incumbents	Challengers
Candidates	10	11
Managers	9	11

Ten candidate-manager pairs were Republicans and eleven were Democrats. Among the challengers, in one congressional district the Democratic candidate and his manager were interviewed soon after they had won the primary election. Two weeks later they lost the recount. They were retained in the study along with the candidate and manager who won the recount because at the time of the interview, they each believed themselves to be the legitimate Democratic standard-bearers.

Campaigners for Statewide Office

Five statewide offices are elected in Wisconsin: governor, lieutenant governor, secretary of state, treasurer, and attorney general. Campaigners interviewed were:

	Incumbents	Challengers
Candidates	2	5
Managers	2	7

Interview Procedures

During the campaign period, the 57 respondents were interviewed and then administered a written personality test. One week after the election, they were sent the post-election questionnaires. In the following interview schedule, changes that were made for managers are in parentheses. Other optional changes are shown in brackets.

1. First, let me ask about your campaign: Do you feel that campaigning makes a difference in whether a candidate wins or loses, or is the election decided by things which you can't control?

2. Are you pretty sure how well you'll (he'll) do when the votes are in, or are you more uncertain about that?

3. Would you be satisfied if you (he) won but just barely, or would you rather (have him) win big? Why is that?

4. What methods do you use [or plan to use] to get your campaign across to the voters?

4a. How much do you use newspaper advertising?

4b. How much do you use campaign literature or newsletters?

4c. How much do you use radio and television?

4d. How much do you use rallies, personal appearances, and things like that?

4e. Which of these methods do you rely on most?

5. *Ask People Who Have Campaigned Before:*

Have you used the same methods before in your campaigns, or are you doing something differently this time? Why, or why not?

Ask New Campaigners:

What previous experience have you had in politics?

6. How do you go about finding how well your campaign is doing in getting people to vote for you?

6a. Do you use any surveys or polls?

If yes:

(1) Who conducts the polls?

(2) Do they ask people anything more than who they're going to vote for? If so, what?

(3) Are the polls done by mail, or phone, or what?

(4) About how many people are polled?

(5) How many polls do you plan to take during the campaign?

6b. Do you ask anyone in particular whether your campaign activities are influencing voters? How much do you rely on them?

6c. Do you ask people who are very active in the party in this area whether your campaign activities are influencing voters? How much do you rely on them?

6d. Do you ask people in the state party organization? How much do you rely on them?

6e. Do you ask any political reporters for newspapers . . . ? How much do you rely on them?

7. Can you tell me any changes you've made in your campaign as a result of what you've heard from any of these people?

If not, would you consider making any changes on the basis of these people's suggestions?

If so, would you make a change in basic strategy, or a more minor one?

8. How much of the time you spend on the campaign is spent in strategy-planning, as opposed to going out and campaigning: most, some, none?

9. Now let's turn to the campaign staff [the people working in your headquarters and helping with the campaign]; Thinking back before you started campaigning:

For People Who Have Run Before:

9a. About how many people are working with your staff for the first time in this campaign, roughly?

9b. When you choose your campaign staff, do you choose good friends (of the candidate), or staffers from your office [political associates], or people active in the party?

9c. Do you have a clear chain of command on the staff, with each person doing an assigned job, or do you have a more informal staff?

For People Running for the First Time:

9d. When you chose your campaign staff, did you choose good friends (of the candidate), or people active in the party, or what?

9e. Do you have a clear chain of command on the staff, with each person doing an assigned job, or do you have a more informal staff?

10. Do you have any professional advisers, like a public relations firm or an advertising agency?

If so, do they actively suggest things to be done in the campaign or do they more or less carry out your (the candidate's) orders?

If not, How useful do you think an ad agency is in winning elections?

11. *Candidates Only:* Since the campaign period is so long, do you do anything in particular to keep up enthusiasm among your campaign workers as the campaign goes along?

Managers Only: Given the personality of the candidate, what kinds of campaign activities do you think he's best suited for, and what kinds would you urge him to avoid? Do you do anything in particular to keep the candidate's enthusiasm high?

12. In general terms, now, do you think a campaign should primarily educate people about the issues, or should it primarily elect a man to office? Which would you stress more [if undecided]?

13. Which do you think a candidate should concentrate his efforts on: the uncommitted voters, or people who already favor him, or who?

14. We hear a lot about a politician's "image." Which do you think is more important in influencing voters: a candidate's image, or the party he belongs to?

15. Do you think a candidate should stick pretty closely to the strategy he planned before the campaign started, or should he be very flexible and respond to events as they happen? *Probe for undecided respondents:* If you had to lean toward one or the other, which would it be?

16. Are there any kinds of campaign activities or appeals to voters which you think are improper in a campaign?

17. Very briefly, now, what are the one or two main issues that you're emphasizing (that are being emphasized) in this campaign?

      17a.   How do you find out how the voters feel about .... [issue mentioned as most important]? Do you check with any specific groups or people to find out? Do you look at surveys?

18. What kinds of issues do you think the contributors to the campaign are most concerned about?

19. Let's imagine for a minute that you (the candidate) decided not to say anything about .... [issue mentioned in question 18] in the campaign. Do you think some people might be less inclined to contribute to the campaign if you (he) weren't talking about .... [the issue mentioned above]?

20. Is there anything you especially dislike about campaigning?

21. Do you have a good idea what your opponent's plans for the campaign are? How much do you take your opponent's actions into account when you plan for your own campaign?

22. How do you go about financing your campaign? What kinds of people do you turn to? Do you turn to any specific groups?

23. Do you have a very good idea which campaign expenditures help you to win the election and which ones may not?

      23a.   Can you think of anything you could cut from your budget without losing any votes?

24. Do you think that it's *good* for a campaigner to be worried about whether he's going to win?

25. Do you have any college students working on your campaign? Do you think college students will be effective campaign workers in this election, or will they produce some negative reactions?

At the end of each interview the following written questions were given to the campaigner.

[Personality Test]

Indicate how much you agree or disagree with each of the following statements by making a check mark on the line below each one. The closer you check to Number 1, the more you agree with the statement; the closer to Number 7, the more you disagree.

Agree Most   1   2   3   4   5   6   7   Disagree Most

1. There is really no such thing as a problem which can't be solved.

  1   2   3   4   5   6   7

2. It is more fun to tackle a complicated problem than to solve a simple one.

  1   2   3   4   5   6   7

3. Many of our most important decisions are based on insufficient information.

  1   2   3   4   5   6   7

4. A person who leads an even, regular life in which few surprises or unexpected happenings arise, really has a lot to be grateful for.

  1   2   3   4   5   6   7

5. A good job is one where what is to be done and how it is to be done are always clear.

  1   2   3   4   5   6   7

6. Often the most interesting and stimulating people are those who don't mind being different and original.

  1   2   3   4   5   6   7

7. In the long run, it is possible to get more done by tackling small, simple problems rather than large and complicated ones.

  1   2   3   4   5   6   7

8. I enjoy parties where most of the people are complete strangers more than ones where I know all or most of the people.

  1   2   3   4   5   6   7

Post-Election Questionnaire

1. During the general election campaign, how much did you use each of the following campaign techniques?

	Used a lot	Used some	Didn't use
television advertising	___	___	___
radio advertising	___	___	___
newspaper advertising	___	___	___
brochures	___	___	___
bumperstickers, cartops, etc.	___	___	___
candidate's personal appearances	___	___	___
canvassing by volunteers	___	___	___

2. If the campaign had had UNLIMITED funds, would you have used more, or less, or the same amount of each technique you actually used?

	Use more	About the same	Use less
television advertising	___	___	___
radio advertising	___	___	___
newspaper advertising	___	___	___
brochures	___	___	___
bumperstickers, cartops, etc.	___	___	___
candidate's personal appearances	___	___	___
canvassing by volunteers	___	___	___

3. Looking back over your own campaign, can you think of any changes you would like to have made:

in the way the campaign was organized?

in the issues that were emphasized?

in any other part of the campaign?

4. Do you feel, in your particular race, that the voters were most influenced by:

_____ the images of the candidates?
_____ the issues of the campaign?
_____ the voters' party preferences?

Notes

Notes

Chapter 1
Introduction

1. See, for example, Angus Campbell et al., *The American Voter* (New York: Wiley, 1960), Chapter 6, pp. 120-145.

2. Joseph A. Schumpeter, *Capitalism, Socialism, and Democracy*, 3rd Ed. (New York: Harper, 1950), p. 285. Others who share the view that the major defining characteristics of democracy are the electorate's ability to freely choose leaders and free competition among prospective leaders include Robert A. Dahl and Charles E. Lindblom, *Politics, Economics and Welfare* (New York: Harper, 1953); Anthony Downs, *An Economic Theory of Democracy* (New York: Harper, 1957); Robert A. Dahl, "Power, Pluralism, and Democracy: A Modest Proposal," paper delivered at the 1964 American Political Science Association annual convention, Chicago; and Jack Dennis, "Support for the Institution of Elections by the Mass Public," *American Political Science Review*, vol. 64 (September, 1970), pp. 819-835. Other writers have suggested that democracy is maintained because the leaders express strong adherence to democratic norms. Exponents of this view are Herbert McClosky, "Consensus and Ideology in American Politics," *American Political Science Review*, vol. 58 (June, 1964), pp. 361-382, and Samuel A. Stouffer, *Communism, Conformity, and Civil Liberties* (Garden City, New York: Doubleday, 1955). Robert W. Jackman in "Political Elites, Mass Publics, and Support for Democratic Principles," *Journal of Politics*, vol. 34 (August, 1972), pp. 753-773, cautions, however, that this conclusion means only that leaders tend to be more educated than most citizens, and education is associated with expressions of support for democratic norms. A third school of thought maintains that democracy is preserved by the network of organizational memberships (and resulting cross-pressures) of American society. See Robert A. Dahl, *Who Governs?* (New Haven: Yale University Press, 1961) and William Kornhauser, *The Politics of Mass Society* (New York: The Free Press, 1959).

3. Schumpeter, op. cit., pp. 279, 282.

4. Frank J. Sorauf, *Party Politics in America*, 2nd Ed. (Boston: Little, Brown, 1972), p. 57.

5. Peter Bachrach, *The Theory of Democratic Elitism, A Critique* (Boston: Little, Brown, 1967), pp. 7, 32.

6. Ibid., 103. See also Jack L. Walker, "A Critique of the Elitist Theory of Democracy," *American Political Science Review*, vol. 60 (June, 1966), pp. 285-295, and Carole Pateman, *Participation and Democratic Theory* (Cambridge: Cambridge University Press, 1970).

7. Bachrach, op. cit., p. 1.

8. Congressional Quarterly, *Current American Government* (Washington, D.C.: Spring, 1971), p. 7. The congressional system reinforces this tendency by rewarding those members who succeed in eliminating serious competition. The advantages of seniority, which are considerable for a congressman, are extended to his constituents in the form of special favors that a senior member is in a position to bestow. In many elections, then, the incumbent's seniority can be a powerful argument for extending that seniority. Voters are asked to ignore the existence of competition. And in some cases there is no competition. From 1966 to 1972, an average of 52 seats in the House of Representatives was not contested. On the advantages of incumbency, see David A. Leuthold, *Election-eering in a Democracy* (New York: Wiley, 1968) and Robert S. Erikson, "The Advantage of Incumbency in Congressional Elections," *Polity*, vol. 3 (Spring, 1971), pp. 395-405.

9. See V.O. Key, Jr., *The Responsible Electorate* (Cambridge: Harvard University Press, 1966).

10. Fred I. Greenstein, *Children and Politics* (New Haven: Yale University Press, 1965), pp. 71-73. Greenstein reports that by the time New Haven school children in his study had reached the fourth grade, 63 percent expressed a party preference, compared with about 75 percent of adults. Other researchers place the development of party identification somewhat later and show higher levels of political independence. See Robert D. Hess and Judith V. Torney, *The Development of Political Attitudes in Children* (Chicago: Aldine, 1967), p. 90.

11. In 1970 the Survey Research Center asked its 1507 respondents to describe the positions of the Democratic and Republican parties on eight key issues of the congressional campaign. For each issue, nearly one-fifth of the respondents could not guess what the party's position was. And given a scale representing two opposing views on an issue and the gradations of opinion between them, another quarter of those respondents expressing an opinion placed the party on the exact midpoint of the scale: the middle-of-the-road position. Relatively few saw enough distance between the two parties to enable them to draw firm distinctions between the parties' positions. Perhaps this reflects the respondents' lack of interest in politics. Or it may indicate that the parties are often seen as repositories for a wide spectrum of political opinions.

12. Lewis Anthony Dexter, "The Representative and His District," *Human Organization*, vol. 16 (Spring, 1957), pp. 2-13. See also Raymond A. Bauer, Ithiel de Sola Pool, and Lewis Anthony Dexter, *American Business and Public Policy* (New York: Atherton, 1963), chapters 29-30.

13. John C. Wahlke et al., *The Legislative System* (New York: Wiley, 1962) p. 281.

14. Roger H. Davidson, *The Role of the Congressman* (Indianapolis: Pegasus 1969), pp. 117-121.

15. One recent case is that of public opinion about China. Gallup polls indicate that in October, 1970, 49 percent of the public opposed admitting the

People's Republic of China to the United Nations. A few months later, in May, 1971, after President Nixon's initiative in establishing contact with that nation, only 38 percent maintained their opposition (*Gallup Opinion Index* #76, Princeton, New Jersey, October, 1971, p. 6).

16. Joseph Napolitan, *The Election Game and How to Win It* (Garden City, New York: Doubleday, 1972), p. 15.

17. Ibid., p. 29.

18. See Herbert E. Alexander, ed., *Studies in Money and Politics* (Princeton: Citizens' Research Foundation, 1965 [vol. I] and 1970 [vol. II]); David Adamany, *Financing Politics: Recent Wisconsin Elections* (Madison: University of Wisconsin Press, 1969); and Alexander Heard, *The Costs of Democracy* (Chapel Hill: University of North Carolina Press, 1960).

19. Nelson W. Polsby and Aaron B. Wildavsky, *Presidential Elections*, 3rd Ed. (New York: Scribner, 1971).

20. Walter DeVries and V. Lance Tarrance, *The Ticket Splitter: A New Force in American Politics* (Grand Rapids, Mich.: Eerdmans, 1972); Harold Mendelsohn and Irving Crespi, *Polls, Television, and the New Politics* (Scranton, Pa.: Chandler, 1970); James M. Perry, *The New Politics* (New York: Potter, 1968).

21. For documentation, see V.O. Key, Jr., *Southern Politics in State and Nation* (New York: Vintage Books, 1949), chapter 14, "Nature and Consequences of One-Party Factionalism."

22. Charles O. Jones, "The Role of the Campaign in Congressional Politics," in M. Kent Jennings and L. Harmon Zeigler, eds., *The Electoral Process* (Englewood Cliffs, N.J.: Prentice-Hall, 1966), p. 29, and Polsby and Wildavsky, op. cit., p. 182.

23. Downs, op. cit., p. 89.

24. Polsby and Wildavsky, op. cit., p. 206. See also Karl A. Lamb and Paul A. Smith, *Campaign Decision-Making* (Belmont, Cal.: Wadsworth, 1968), p. 30.

25. Leuthold, op. cit.

26. Polsby and Wildavsky, op. cit., pp. 172-175.

27. See, for example, Murray B. Levin, *The Compleat Politician: Political Strategy in Massachusetts* (Indianapolis: Bobbs-Merrill, 1962) and Lamb and Smith, op. cit.

28. Theodore H. White, *The Making of the President 1968* (New York: Pocket Books, 1970), pp. 287, 159, and 354.

29. V.O. Key, Jr., *Politics, Parties, and Pressure Groups*, 5th Ed. (New York: Crowell, 1964), p. 457.

30. Levin, op. cit., p. 271.

31. Napolitan, op. cit., pp. 17-18.

32. John H. Kessel, "A Game Theory Analysis of Campaign Strategy," in Jennings and Zeigler, op. cit., pp. 300-301.

33. John W. Kingdon, *Candidates for Office: Beliefs and Strategies* (New York: Random House, 1966), pp. 52, 103-104.

34. Leon D. Epstein, *Politics in Wisconsin* (Madison: University of Wisconsin Press, 1958), pp. 30-31, 77, 83, and 88. An excellent description of amateur organizations is given in James Q. Wilson's *The Amateur Democrat* (Chicago: University of Chicago Press, 1962).

35. Epstein, op. cit., pp. 37-44.

36. Using a composite index of the popular vote for Democratic candidates for governor, the percentage of Democratic state legislative seats, and the percentage of all gubernatorial and state legislative terms controlled by Democrats, Austin Ranney ranked the states, averaging the percentages, from 1.000 (wholly Democratic) to .000 (wholly Republican). Wisconsin, ranked .4102, fell into the two-party category. Data covered the years 1956-1970. (Austin Ranney, "Parties in State Politics," in Herbert Jacob and Kenneth N. Vines, eds., *Politics in the American States*, 2nd Ed. (Boston: Little, Brown, 1971), p. 87.

37. Ibid., p. 91.

38. "The Fight for the 69," *Time*, vol. 96 (October 12, 1970), pp. 16-17. Reprinted by permission from *Time*, The Weekly Newsmagazine; Copyright Time Inc.

39. Richard M. Scammon and Ben J. Wattenberg, *The Real Majority* (New York: Coward-McCann, 1970).

40. Dave Zweifel, *The Capital Times* (Madison, Wisconsin), November 5, 1970, p. 4.

41. Kingdon, op. cit., pp. 22-27.

Chapter 2
How Uncertainty Affects
Campaign Decision-Making

1. James Bryce, *Modern Democracies* (New York: Macmillan, 1921), vol. II (*Some Democracies in their Working*), p. 19.

2. Edward C. Dreyer and Walter A. Rosenbaum, "Political Opinion and Public Policy," in their *Political Opinion and Electoral Behavior* (Belmont, Cal.: Wadsworth, 1966), p. 383.

3. Angus Campbell et al., *The American Voter* (New York: Wiley, 1960), chapter 2, pp. 42-63. See also Donald E. Stokes and Warren E. Miller, "Party Government and the Saliency of Congress," *Public Opinion Quarterly*, vol. 26 (Winter, 1962), pp. 531-546, and Warren E. Miller and Donald E. Stokes, "Constituency Influence in Congress," *American Political Science Review*, vol. 57 (March, 1963), pp. 53-54.

4. These data, broken down into winners and losers, can be found in John W. Kingdon, *Candidates for Office: Beliefs and Strategies* (New York: Random House, 1966), pp. 23, 26. The combined data, cited above, are found in Kingdon's *Candidates for Office*, unpublished Ph.D. thesis, University of Wisconsin, 1965, pp. 62, 69-71.

5. Stokes and Miller, op. cit., p. 542.

6. Miller and Stokes, op. cit., pp. 54-55. See also Robert S. Erikson, "The Electoral Impact of Congressional Roll Call Voting," *American Political Science Review*, vol. 65 (December, 1971), pp. 1031-1032.

7. Murray Edelman, *The Symbolic Uses of Politics* (Urbana: University of Illinois Press, 1964), p. 3.

8. Charles O. Jones, "The Role of the Campaign in Congressional Politics," in M. Kent Jennings and L. Harmon Zeigler, eds., *The Electoral Process* (Englewood Cliffs, N.J.: Prentice-Hall, 1966), p. 29.

9. David A. Leuthold, *Electioneering in a Democracy* (New York: Wiley, 1968), pp. 75-76.

10. Nelson W. Polsby and Aaron B. Wildavsky, *Presidential Elections*, 3rd Ed. (New York: Scribner, 1971), p. 206.

11. Karl A. Lamb and Paul A. Smith, *Campaign Decision-Making* (Belmont, Cal.: Wadsworth, 1968), p. 30.

12. Charles L. Clapp, *The Congressman: His Work As He Sees It* (Washington: Brookings, 1963), pp. 351 and 379.

13. Anthony Downs, *An Economic Theory of Democracy* (New York: Harper, 1957), p. 13.

14. Richard M. Cyert and James G. March, *A Behavioral Theory of the Firm* (Englewood Cliffs, N.J.: Prentice-Hall, 1963), p. 119.

15. Kingdon, *Candidates for Office: Beliefs and Strategies*, p. 89.

16. Harold D. Lasswell, *Psychopathology and Politics*, 2nd Ed. (New York: Viking Press, 1960), pp. 50, 75-76.

17. See Robert E. Lane, *Political Life* (Glencoe: The Free Press, 1959), pp. 126-128.

Chapter 3
Personalities in Campaigns:
The Effects of Tolerance of
Ambiguity

1. Murray B. Levin, *Kennedy Campaigning* (Boston: Beacon Press, 1966), p. 42.

2. Ernest R. Hilgard, *Introduction to Psychology*, 3rd Ed. (New York: Harcourt, Brace & World, 1962), p. 447.

3. Barber argues that "Initial political candidacy represents a marked shift in the continuity of the person's regular life at work, in the home and community, a shift not clearly evaluated by general cultural norms nor clearly guided by special norms." The candidate is thus exposed to much more intense personal strain than if he were involved in politics in a less active way. A person with high self-esteem is likely to have the personal resources to deal with this sudden increase in problems. Alternatively, a person with fairly low self-esteem

may compensate for the increase in stress by finding other satisfactions. Since, according to Barber, campaigning requires an individual to manage these strains, and since fairly high or fairly low self-esteem can be helpful in this task, political candidacy tends to attract people with these resources. (James David Barber, *The Lawmakers: Recruitment and Adaptation to Legislative Life* (New Haven: Yale University Press, 1965), p. 225.)

4. John B. McConaughy, "Certain Personality Factors of State Legislators in South Carolina," *American Political Science Review*, vol. 44 (December, 1950), pp. 897-903.

5. Rufus P. Browning and Herbert Jacob, "Power Motivation and the Political Personality," *Public Opinion Quarterly*, vol. 28 (Spring, 1964), pp. 85, 88-89.

6. Karl A. Lamb and Paul A. Smith, *Campaign Decision-Making* (Belmont, Cal.: Wadsworth, 1968), p. 49.

7. Murray B. Levin, *The Compleat Politician: Political Strategy in Massachusetts* (Indianapolis: Bobbs-Merrill, 1962), pp. 289 and 293.

8. Reported in Herbert McClosky, "Conservatism and Personality," *American Political Science Review*, vol. 52 (March, 1958), p. 44 (data not shown).

9. David O. Sears, "Political Behavior," in Gardner Lindzey and Elliot Aronson, Eds., *Handbook of Social Psychology*, 2nd Ed., vol. V (Reading, Mass.: Addison-Wesley, 1969), p. 337.

10. Fred I. Greenstein, *Personality and Politics* (Chicago: Markham, 1969), pp. 50-61.

11. Stanley Budner, "Intolerance of Ambiguity as a Personality Variable," *Journal of Personality* vol. 30 (March, 1962), p. 29.

12. John P. Robinson and Phillip R. Shaver, *Measures of Social Psychological Attitudes* (Ann Arbor: Survey Research Center, Institute for Social Research, 1969), p. 319. Else Frenkel-Brunswik also supports this conclusion in "Intolerance of Ambiguity as an Emotional and Perceptual Personality Variable," *Journal of Personality*, vol. 18 (1949), pp. 108-143.

13. Bernard R. Berelson et al., *Voting* (Chicago: University of Chicago Press, 1954), pp. 217-222.

14. See, for example, Leon Festinger, *A Theory of Cognitive Dissonance* (Evanston: Row, Peterson, 1957).

15. Jack W. Brehm and Arthur R. Cohen, *Explorations in Cognitive Dissonance* (New York: Wiley, 1962), pp. 206-210.

16. Raymond E. Wolfinger and Fred I. Greenstein, "The Repeal of Fair Housing in California: An Analysis of Referendum Voting," *American Political Science Review*, vol. 62 (September, 1968), pp. 753-769. See also Denis G. Sullivan, "Psychological Balance and Reactions to the Presidential Nominations in 1960," in M. Kent Jennings and L. Harmon Zeigler, eds., *The Electoral Process* (Englewood Cliffs, N.J.: Prentice-Hall, 1966), pp. 238-264.

17. John W. Kingdon, "Politicians' Beliefs about Voters," *American Political Science Review*, vol. 61 (March, 1967), pp. 137-145.

18. Walter DeVries and V. Lance Tarrance, *The Ticket-Splitter: A New Force in American Politics* (Grand Rapids, Mich.: Eerdmans, 1972), p. 74.

19. Lamb and Smith, op. cit., pp. 20-35.

20. Ibid., p. 19.

21. Herbert McClosky et al., "Issue Conflict and Consensus Among Party Leaders and Followers," *American Political Science Review*, vol. 54 (June, 1960), pp. 406-427.

22. Chong Lim Kim, "Political Attitudes of Defeated Candidates in an American State Election," *American Political Science Review*, vol. 64 (September, 1970), pp. 879-887.

Chapter 4
Organization and Disorganization

1. For a discussion of the political party as a social group and a political system, see Samuel J. Eldersveld, *Political Parties: A Behavioral Analysis* (Chicago: Rand McNally, 1964), pp. 1-13.

2. Karl A. Lamb and Paul A. Smith in *Campaign Decision-Making* (Belmont, Cal.: Wadsworth, 1968) contrast the highly structured Goldwater organization with the more informal Johnson campaign. In Theodore H. White's *The Making of the President 1968* (New York: Pocket Books, 1970) the businesslike Nixon staff is shown in comparison with the disorganized Humphrey campaign.

3. See, for example, Rowland Evans, Jr., and Robert D. Novak, *Nixon in the White House* (New York: Vintage, 1972).

4. The classic statement of the tendency toward oligarchy in organizations, including political parties, is Robert Michels, *Political Parties* (London: Collier-Macmillan, 1962). On the question of intraparty democracy see Austin Ranney, *The Doctrine of Responsible Party Government* (Urbana: University of Illinois Press, 1962), and Samuel J. Eldersveld, op. cit., chapter 5. Eldersveld suggests that party oligarchy is prevented by sheer organizational confusion, plus the need of party leaders for the support of their subordinates.

5. Talcott Parsons, *Sociological Theory and Modern Society* (New York: The Free Press, 1967), pp. 9, 145.

6. See David A. Leuthold, *Electioneering in a Democracy* (New York: Wiley, 1968) and Hugh Scott, *How to Run for Public Office, and Win!* (Washington: The National Press, Inc., 1968).

7. See Nelson W. Polsby and Aaron B. Wildavsky, *Presidential Elections*, 3rd Ed. (New York: Scribner, 1971), p. 191, and Ira Sharkansky, *The Routines of Politics* (New York: Van Nostrand Reinhold, 1970), pp. 20, 137.

8. Sharkansky, idem.

9. Austin Ranney and Willmoore Kendall, *Democracy and the American Party System* (New York: Harcourt Brace, 1956), chapter 15.

10. See Marion J. Levy, Jr., *The Structure of Society* (Princeton: Princeton University Press, 1952), p. 114.

11. See Lewis A. Froman, Jr., "A Realistic Approach to Campaign Strategies and Tactics," in M. Kent Jennings and L. Harmon Zeigler, eds., *The Electoral Process* (Englewood Cliffs, N.J.: Prentice-Hall, 1966), pp. 8, 11. Also see Polsby and Wildavsky, op. cit., p. 9.

12. See Dan Nimmo, *The Political Persuaders* (Englewood Cliffs, N.J.: Prentice-Hall, 1970), p. 119.

13. Idem.

14. See, for example, Walter DeVries and V. Lance Tarrance, *The Ticket-Splitter: A New Force in American Politics* (Grand Rapids, Mich.: Eerdmans, 1972).

15. John H. Kessel, *The Goldwater Coalition* (Indianapolis: Bobbs-Merrill, 1968), p. 131.

16. John W. Kingdon, "Politicians' Beliefs about Voters," *American Political Science Review*, vol. 61 (March, 1967), pp. 139-140.

17. See, for example, chapter VI in Harold D. Lasswell, *Psychopathology and Politics*, 2nd Ed. (New York: Viking, 1960).

18. Robert E. Lane, *Political Life* (Glencoe: The Free Press, 1959), pp. 115-124.

19. Leuthold, op. cit., p. 108 (note 8).

20. Ibid., pp. 106-107.

21. Many writers state that politicians believe campaigns are all-important to their political futures. See, for example, Nimmo, op. cit., p. 3. In this study, however, the nearness of defeat as well as campaign stress is associated with a tendency to minimize the importance of campaigning. For example, campaigners who would later lose the election were much more likely to consider the campaign relatively unimportant to the election result (gammas are .68 for candidates, .23 for managers).

22. Eldersveld, op. cit., pp. 9-10.

Chapter 5
Influences on the Roles
Campaigners Play

1. Roger H. Davidson, *The Role of the Congressman* (Indianapolis: Pegasus, 1969), p. 73. Davidson looks at the role cognitions of a sample of U.S. congressmen during the 1963-64 session.

2. John W. Thibaut and Harold H. Kelley, *The Social Psychology of Groups* (New York: Wiley, 1959), p. 148. See also Bruce J. Biddle and Edwin J. Thomas, eds., *Role Theory: Concepts and Research* (New York: Wiley, 1966), pp. 3-63; and Neal Gross, Ward S. Mason, and Alexander McEachern, *Explorations in Role Analysis* (New York: Wiley, 1958).

3. See Theodore R. Sarbin and Vernon L. Allen, "Role Theory," in Gardner

Lindzey and Elliot Aronson, eds., *The Handbook of Social Psychology*, 2nd Ed. (Reading, Mass.: Addison-Wesley, 1968), vol. I, pp. 488-567.

4. See, for example, the discussion of voters' perceptions about legislative and judicial roles at the federal, state and local levels in Carl D. McMurray and Malcolm B. Parsons, "Public Attitudes Toward the Representational Roles of Legislators and Judges," *Midwest Journal of Political Science*, vol. 9 (May, 1965), pp. 167-185. Their sample consisted of 207 white residents of Florida's Cape Kennedy area.

5. Lewis Bowman and G.R. Boynton, "Activities and Role Definitions of Grassroots Party Officials," *Journal of Politics*, vol. 28 (February, 1966), p. 125.

6. Davidson, op. cit., p. 78.

7. Ibid., p. 74. See also John C. Wahlke et al., *The Legislative System* (New York: Wiley, 1962), p. 12.

8. See Davidson's chapter 4, pp. 110-142.

9. Ibid., p. 97.

10. Bowman and Boynton, op. cit., pp. 133-134.

11. See, for example, Kenneth Prewitt and Alan Stone, *The Ruling Elites* (New York: Harper & Row, 1973), chapter 8, pp. 184-223; Hanna Fenichel Pitkin, *The Concept of Representation* (Berkeley: University of California Press, 1967); Warren E. Miller and Donald E. Stokes, "Constituency Influence in Congress," *American Political Science Review*, vol. 57 (March, 1963), pp. 45-56; and Gerald M. Pomper, *Elections in America* (New York: Dodd, Mead, 1971).

12. Davidson, op. cit., p. 74. Examples of such consensual roles are found in Donald R. Matthews, *U.S. Senators and Their World*, 2nd Ed. (New York: W.W. Norton & Co., 1973), chapter 5, "The Folkways of the Senate."

13. Lewis A. Froman, Jr., "A Realistic Approach to Campaign Strategies and Tactics," in M. Kent Jennings and L. Harmon Zeigler, eds., *The Electoral Process* (Englewood Cliffs, N.J.: Prentice-Hall, 1966), p. 11.

14. Nelson W. Polsby and Aaron B. Wildavsky, *Presidential Elections*, 3rd Ed. (New York: Scribner, 1971), pp. 172-175.

15. Samuel J. Eldersveld, *Political Parties: A Behavioral Analysis* (Chicago: Rand McNally, 1964), p. 254.

16. John W. Kingdon, *Candidates for Office: Beliefs and Strategies* (New York: Random House, 1966), p. 59.

17. Davidson, op. cit., p. 130.

18. Samuel C. Patterson, "Characteristics of Party Leaders," *Western Political Quarterly*, vol. 16 (June, 1963), pp. 350-352 (a study of county party leaders).

19. James M. Perry, *The New Politics* (New York: Potter, 1968), p. 215.

20. See, for example, the argument in Robert E. Lane and David O. Sears, *Public Opinion* (Englewood Cliffs, N.J.: Prentice-Hall, 1964), pp. 28-32.

21. See Joseph A. Schlesinger, "Lawyers and American Politics: A Clarified View," *Midwest Journal of Political Science*, vol. 1 (May, 1957), pp. 26-39;

David R. Derge, "The Lawyer as Decision-Maker in the American State Legislature," *Journal of Politics*, vol. 21 (August, 1959), pp. 408-433, and Heinz Eulau and John D. Sprague, *Lawyers in Politics* (Indianapolis: Bobbs-Merrill, 1964).

22. See Herbert Jacob, "Initial Recruitment of Elected Officials in the U.S.—A Model," *Journal of Politics,* vol. 24 (November, 1962), pp. 709-710.

23. See Kingdon, op. cit., pp. 110, 112; and Charles O. Jones, "The Role of the Campaign in Congressional Politics," in Jennings and Zeigler, op. cit., p. 29.

24. See Robert S. Erikson, "The Advantage of Incumbency in Congressional Elections," *Polity*, vol. 3 (Spring, 1971), pp. 395-405.

25. Charles L. Clapp, *The Congressman: His Work As He Sees It* (Washington: Brookings, 1963), p. 331.

26. Ibid., p. 372.

27. Davidson, op. cit., p. 140, proposes that representational roles "are largely extensions of the member's electoral safety or vulnerability."

28. Erving Goffman, *The Presentation of Self in Everyday Life* (Garden City, N.Y.: Doubleday, 1959), p. 72.

29. Karl A. Lamb and Paul A. Smith describe the strength of such unwritten rules in presidential campaigns. See *Campaign Decision-Making* (Bemont, Cal.: Wadsworth, 1968), pp. 156, 165.

30. Joe McGinniss, *The Selling of the President 1968* (New York: Trident, 1969), p. 23.

Chapter 6
Conclusion

1. This is one of the two models of management described by Douglas McGregor in *The Human Side of Enterprise* (New York: McGraw-Hill, 1960), pp. 33-57. McGregor's "theory X" and "theory Y" contrast a hard-line hierarchical management approach with a more humanistic style directed at producing voluntary involvement by workers. McGregor believes that a leader's personality and attitudes condition his acceptance of theory X or theory Y.

2. Goldwater's campaign is described by Karl A. Lamb and Paul A. Smith in *Campaign Decision-Making* (Belmont, Cal.: Wadsworth, 1968), pp. 50 and 54.

3. Ibid., pp. 20-29.

4. Ibid., pp. 144-150.

5. Most political leaders probably identify their own success with the success of the nation. But politicians differ in the extent to which they are willing to bend or break the rules of the game to achieve success, and in the extent to which they can accept the idea that other factors, in addition to their success, are vital to national progress. See, for example, the discussion of politicians and the national interest in Bruce Mazlish, *In Search of Nixon*

(Baltimore: Penguin, 1973), pp. 85-87; and David Wise's *The Politics of Lying* (New York: Random House, 1973), chapters 9 through 13.

6. See, for example, the perceptive study by James David Barber, *The Presidential Character, Predicting Performance in the White House* (Englewood Cliffs, N.J.: Prentice-Hall, 1972).

7. See Robert D. Hess and Judith V. Torney, *The Development of Political Attitudes in Children* (Chicago: Aldine, 1967), pp. 82-83; and Dean Jaros, *Socialization to Politics* (New York: Praeger, 1973), p. 70.

8. See, for example, William C. Mitchell, "The Ambivalent Social Status of the American Politician," *Western Political Quarterly*, vol. 12 (September, 1959), pp. 692-695.

9. Samuel J. Eldersveld in *Political Parties: A Behavioral Analysis* (Chicago: Rand McNally, 1964), pp. 530-532, suggests that participating in the party organization affects workers' motivation for party work, their awareness of party goals, their career aspirations, and their task efficiency. So the party organization, and the campaign, can be an independent variable as well as a dependent variable.

10. This unstructured, nonhierarchical style of campaigning can also be seen in national races. For example, see the description of the 1972 presidential campaign of George McGovern by his press secretary, Richard Dougherty, in *Goodbye, Mr. Christian* (Garden City, New York: Doubleday, 1973).

11. This framework is described in Harry Eckstein, "A Theory of Stable Democracy," Appendix B in Eckstein's *Division and Cohesion in Democracy* (Princeton: Princeton University Press, 1966), pp. 239-241.

12. For discussions of role learning, see Henry Clay Lindgren, *An Introduction to Social Psychology* (New York: Wiley, 1969), pp. 159-178; B.F. Skinner, *Science and Human Behavior* (New York: Macmillan, 1953); and Albert Bandura and Richard H. Walters, *Social Learning and Personality Development* (New York: Holt, Rinehart & Winston, 1963).

13. Murray B. Levin, *The Compleat Politician: Political Strategy in Massachusetts* (Indianapolis: Bobbs-Merrill, 1962), p. 242; and Stanley Kelley, Jr., *Professional Public Relations and Political Power* (Baltimore: Johns Hopkins, 1966), p. 205.

14. Dan Nimmo, *The Political Persuaders* (Englewood Cliffs, N.J.: Prentice-Hall, 1970), pp. 65-66.

15. Kelley, op. cit., pp. 187-191.

16. See, for example, the work of Jack L. Walker, "The Diffusion of Innovations among the American States," *American Political Science Review,* vol. 63 (September, 1969), pp. 880-899. See also Everett M. Rogers, *Communication of Innovations; a cross-cultural approach*, 2nd Ed. (New York: Free Press, 1971); and Gerald Zaltman, Robert Duncan and Jonny Holbek, *Innovations and Organizations* (New York: Wiley, 1973).

Appendix

1. Interest in the effects of uncertainty and theories of campaigning was stimulated by John W. Kingdon's *Candidates for Office: Beliefs and Strategies* (New York: Random House, 1966) and his "Politicians' Beliefs about Voters," *American Political Science Review*, vol. 61 (March, 1967), pp. 137-145. Karl A. Lamb and Paul A. Smith's *Campaign Decision-Making* (Belmont, Cal.: Wadsworth, 1968) led to a concern with campaigners' personality traits, as did *Influencing Voters* by Richard Rose (New York: St. Martin's, 1967). Initial interest in the relationship between stress and politics stemmed from Harold D. Lasswell's *Psychopathology and Politics*, 2nd Ed. (New York: Viking, 1960). David A. Leuthold's *Electioneering in a Democracy* (New York: Wiley, 1968) prompted a study of the effects of incumbency. No hypotheses about candidate-manager differences had been developed before the interviewing. During meetings with campaigners, however, these differences quickly became apparent.

2. John P. Robinson and Phillip R. Shaver, *Measures of Social Psychological Attitudes* (Ann Arbor: Survey Research Center, Institute for Social Research, 1969).

3. Stanley Budner, "Intolerance of Ambiguity as a Personality Variable," *Journal of Personality*, vol. 30 (March, 1962), pp. 33-35.

4. Ibid., p. 29.

5. Robinson and Shaver, op. cit., p. 319.

6. Budner, op. cit., p. 35.

7. Jack Block and Jeanne Block, "An Investigation of the Relationship Between Intolerance of Ambiguity and Ethnocentrism," *Journal of Personality*, vol. 19 (1951), pp. 303-311.

8. John Kingdon contends (op. cit., pp. 52, 103-104) that candidates for state legislative office were not as concerned about strategy, had less information about the campaign situation, and felt less in control of the circumstances of the campaign than did candidates for higher-level offices. It was assumed that choosing the more competitive state legislative races would bridge some of the differences between the two levels of offices.

9. This technique is similar to that of Sanford I. Labovitz in "Methods for Control with Small Sample Size," *American Sociological Review*, vol. 30 (April, 1965), pp. 243-249.

10. Lewis Anthony Dexter, "Role Relationships and Conceptions of Neutrality in Interviewing," *American Journal of Sociology*, vol. 62 (September, 1956), p. 153.

11. Ibid., p. 155. Reprinted by permission of the publisher, © 1956 University of Chicago Press.

12. Idem.

13. See Marjorie Randon Hershey, "Incumbency and the Minimum Winning Coalition," *American Journal of Political Science*, vol. 17 (August, 1973), pp. 631-637.

14. Herbert Hyman, *Survey Design and Analysis* (Glencoe: The Free Press, 1955), pp. 255-256.

15. Leo A. Goodman and William H. Kruskal, "Measures of Association for Cross-Classifications," *Journal of the American Statistical Association*, vol. 49 (December, 1954), pp. 732-764.

16. Herbert L. Costner, "Criteria for Measures of Association," *American Sociological Review*, vol. 30 (June, 1965), p. 344.

17. This standard is similar to that found in Vincent Jeffries and Richard T. Morris, "Altruism, Egoism, and Antagonism Toward Negroes," in Norval D. Glenn and Charles M. Bonjean, eds., *Blacks in the United States* (San Francisco: Chandler, 1969), p. 235, notes 18 and 19.

18. Enrico Federighi, "The Use of Chi-Square in Small Samples," *American Sociological Review*, vol. 15 (December, 1950), pp. 777-779.

19. John C. Wahlke et al., *The Legislative System* (New York: Wiley, 1962), p. 459.

Index

Index

About the Author

Marjorie Hershey studied journalism at the University of Michigan and political science at the University of Wisconsin, where she received the Ph.D. Since 1972 she has been a member of the faculty of the Department of Government and the Institute for Social Research at Florida State University.